Homemade
for the Holidays

A THANKSGIVING & CO COOKBOOK

THANKSGIVING & CO.

Published in the United States by Grateful Ink, a
division of Grateful Ventures.

Thanksgiving & Co and Thanksgiving.com are
owned and operated by Grateful Ventures.

Grateful Ventures is a Gannett Co., Inc. company
and part of the USA TODAY Network.

ISBN: 978-0-692-04166-6

Photography by David Flores
(unless otherwise indicated)

Book design by Tiffany Egbert

Cover photo: Holiday mixed fruit pie, page 192

Welcome to America's Home for the Holidays

Spicy yet sweet aromas, flavorful food and family favorites served alongside fresh flavors. You're invited to take a seat at our table and enjoy America's holidays with us. At Thanksgiving.com, we're America's home for all holidays, not just Thanksgiving (though we are partial to feast that started it all for us!).

We're grateful you've chosen to spend your holiday season with us. We invite you to browse through our favorite recipes and blogger dishes to create a menu for the most memorable and delicious holiday meal yet. Each recipe includes helpful tips from our test kitchen, nutrition information to help you make informed decisions and has been kitchen-tested by our team.

–The Grateful family, home of Thanksgiving.com

TABLE OF CONTENTS

DIETARY KEY

DF DAIRY-FREE	**GR** GRAIN-FREE	**Q** QUICK
EF EGG-FREE	**LC** LOW-CARB	**V** VEGETARIAN
GF GLUTEN-FREE	**NF** NUT-FREE	**VG** VEGAN

Menu Planning

HOLIDAY FOR TWO

Appetizers

Caramelized onion and spinach stuffed mushrooms *(38)*

Garlicky pumpkin hummus *(27)*

Soup & Salad

Slow-cooker roasted garlic baked potato soup *(54)*

Holiday salad with arugula and cranberries *(51)*

Main Course

Rosemary turkey breast *(122)*

Roasted carrots with Indian spices,
creamy dressing & walnut-parsley topping *(114)*

Homemade orange cranberry sauce *(166)*

Honey cinnamon sweet potatoes *(82)*

Best basic dinner rolls *(66)*

Desserts

Sweet potato pie *(186)*

Red velvet cream cheese sandwich cookies *(188)*

Drinks

Amaretto cranberry kiss *(235)*

ELEGANT

Appetizers

Elegant crab dip *(18)*

Tuna tartare with homemade wonton crackers *(28.29)*

Soup & Salad

Creamy onion soup with bacon nut crumble *(53)*

Pear salad with blood orange vinaigrette *(52)*

Main Course

Pan-seared filet mignon with shallot butter *(148)*

Orange anise & thyme roasted turkey *(136)*

Brandied wild rice stuffing with cornbread and pecans *(110)*

Maple brown butter mashed sweet potatoes *(80)*

Maple bacon roasted Brussels sprouts *(112)*

Twisted rosemary breadsticks *(70)*

Desserts

Holiday cheese tart with strawberry glaze *(208)*

Dark chocolate pecan pie *(182)*

Peppermint mocha cookies *(184)*

Drinks

Sweet and fruity faux champagne *(242)*

Simple maple bacon eggnog *(233)*

GLUTEN-FREE

Appetizers

Spinach artichoke deviled eggs *(16)*

Divine guacamole dip *(20)*

Soup & Salad

Slow-cooker roasted garlic baked potato soup *(54)*

Red wine grape, tangerine and wild rice salad *(47)*

Main Course

Easy no-fuss holiday turkey *(134)*

Roasted butternut squash *(116)*

Maple bacon roasted Brussels sprouts *(112)*

Mushroom stuffing *(109)*

Gluten-free cornbread with cherry butter *(74)*

Desserts

Grain-free pecan pie *(201)*

Black bean brownies *(190)*

Drinks

Apple cider sangria *(239)*

Boozy pumpkin white hot chocolate *(243)*

QUICK

Appetizers

Divine guacamole dip *(20)*

Homemade wonton crackers *(28)*

Cheesy prosciutto-wrapped asparagus bundles *(39)*

Salad

Autumn kale and spinach salad *(50)*

Main Course

Grilled salmon with maple and rosemary *(158)*

Apple cranberry sauce *(174)*

Pressure cooker mac and cheese *(102)*

Green beans with crunchy almonds *(94)*

Honey cornbread muffins *(60)*

Desserts

Chocolate-Kahlua snowball cookies *(216)*

No-bake pumpkin pie *(203)*

VEGETARIAN

Appetizers

Baked Brie with blackberry compote and pecans *(24)*

Caramelized onion and spinach stuffed mushrooms *(38)*

Soup & Salad

Celery root, apple and walnut salad *(51)*

Cream of kale soup with Parmesan crisps *(57)*

Main Course

Tofurkey with mushroom stuffing and gravy *(138)*

Balsamic and Parmesan roasted cauliflower *(93)*

Honey butter roasted acorn squash *(118)*

Creamy baked macaroni and cheese *(101)*

Desserts

Truffles three ways *(218)*

Holiday cheese tart with strawberry glaze *(208)*

Drinks

Pumpkin fizz cocktail *(244)*

Dulce de Leche hot chocolate *(246)*

VEGAN

Appetizers

Vegan raw "cheese" sun-dried tomato and pesto spread *(26)*

Garlicky pumpkin hummus *(27)*

Soup & Salad

Vegan cauliflower soup *(55)*

Smoky quinoa black bean salad *(46)*

Main Course

Butternut roast *(162)*

Vegan green bean casserole *(98)*

Grain-free stuffing *(106)*

Desserts

Chocolate-Kahlua snowball cookies *(216)*

Vegan chocolate pecan pie *(196)*

Drinks

Vegan spiced-apple margaritas *(236)*

Pomegranate thyme bubbly rosé *(235)*

Appetizers

SPINACH ARTICHOKE DEVILED EGGS

Spinach and artichokes give this version an earthy, rustic flavor that's perfect for fall.

MAKES: 12 EGGS | PREP 25 MINS | COOK 9 MINS

INGREDIENTS

6 large hard-boiled eggs

2 tablespoons mayonnaise

3 tablespoons plain Greek yogurt

1/2 teaspoon distilled white vinegar

1 teaspoon spicy brown mustard

1/2 teaspoon sugar

1/8 teaspoon salt

1/8 teaspoon ground black pepper

1/8 teaspoon garlic powder

1 pinch cayenne pepper

1/4 cup frozen chopped spinach, thawed and drained

1/4 cup artichoke hearts, cooked and finely chopped

3 teaspoons finely chopped chives, divided

1 pinch paprika

INSTRUCTIONS

1. Prepare ice water bath: Fill large bowl with 4 cups cold water and 4 cups ice. This will help cool eggs quickly after cooking.

2. Place eggs in medium saucepan in single layer; cover with 1 inch cold water.

3. Bring to rapid simmer over high heat (should take about 9 minutes; bubbles should be breaking surface of water quickly). Turn off heat.

4. Drain water from saucepan and gently shake pan back and forth to crack eggshells. Transfer eggs to ice water bath with slotted spoon and let sit for at least 5 minutes.

5. Tap each thoroughly-cooled egg on counter to crack shell. Carefully peel egg, dipping in cool water or holding under running water to help remove shell.

6. Slice peeled eggs in half lengthwise.

7. Transfer yolks to fine-mesh sieve and press through into bowl with rubber spatula.

8. Add mayonnaise, yogurt, vinegar, mustard, sugar, salt, black pepper, garlic powder, cayenne pepper, spinach, artichoke hearts and 1 teaspoon chives. Combine until smooth.

9. Transfer mixture to piping bag or resealable plastic bag. Press mixture into one corner and twist top of bag. Using scissors, cut about 1/2 inch off corner of bag.

10. Arrange whites on serving platter. Squeeze bag to pipe filling into whites, to about 1/2 inch above whites. Sprinkle with paprika and remaining chives.

tip | In addition to reducing your prep time, the ice bath also makes peeling easier.

ELEGANT CRAB DIP

Adding seafood to your holiday appetizer spread balances out the more traditional flavors.

SERVES 6–8 | PREP 25 MINS | COOK 16 MINS

INGREDIENTS

1-1/2 cups French bread, crusts removed and cubed

1 cup whole milk

2 teaspoons butter

1-1/2 teaspoons fresh tarragon, minced

1/2 cup white onion, grated

16 ounces whole lump crabmeat

1/4 cup heavy cream

1/4 teaspoon cayenne pepper

Kosher salt

Freshly ground black pepper

2/3 cup Parmesan cheese, freshly grated

1 baguette, cut into 1/4-inch slices and toasted

INSTRUCTIONS

1. Preheat broiler to 500F.

2. Combine bread and milk in small bowl. Set aside for 5 minutes.

3. Using blender, purée milk and bread until very smooth, then force mixture through fine mesh strainer.

4. In 3-quart saucepan, warm butter over medium-low heat. Add tarragon and sauté gently, just until fragrant and sizzling, about 2 minutes.

5. Add onion and continue sautéeing for 5 to 6 minutes, until onion is translucent and soft.

6. Add crab, cayenne pepper and milk mixture to pan, then stir gently until thoroughly combined and warm.

7. Remove pan from stove and fold in heavy cream.

8. Season to taste with salt and pepper.

9. Transfer crab mixture to serving dish. Evenly cover dip with grated Parmesan cheese and broil for 5 minutes.

10. Allow crab dip to rest for 5 minutes before serving with toasted baguette.

DIVINE GUACAMOLE DIP

Turn traditional guacamole into fall fare with the addition of crunchy "pepitas" (pumpkin seeds!).

SERVES 4–6 | PREP 20 MINS

INGREDIENTS

4 ripe avocados, peeled and seeded, skin removed, cut into chunks

3 garlic cloves, finely minced

1 serrano pepper, seeds removed and finely diced

Half an onion, finely diced

1 Roma tomato, finely diced

2 tablespoons freshly squeezed lime juice

1 teaspoon sea salt (to taste)

Freshly grated pepper (to taste)

1/4 cup pepitas, toasted

INSTRUCTIONS

1. Place avocado flesh in large bowl. Add minced garlic, serrano pepper, grated onion, tomato, lime juice, salt and pepper.

2. Mash with potato masher, leaving some chunkiness.

3. Taste and adjust seasonings.

4. Garnish with toasted pepitas.

smart swap / Swap chips for sliced vegetables if you want to keep this appetizer lighter before your feast.

MINI 7-LAYER DIPS

Spice up your next fall get-together with these individual dips.

SERVES 8 | PREP 30 MINS

INGREDIENTS

One 16-ounce can refried beans

1 ounce taco seasoning

1 cup homemade guacamole

8 ounces sour cream

1 cup pico de gallo

1 cup cheddar cheese, shredded

2 Roma tomatoes, diced

1/2 bunch scallions, sliced

1 can (2-1/4 ounces) black olives, drained and sliced

Eight 9-ounce clear plastic cups

Tortilla chips

INSTRUCTIONS

1. In small bowl, mix taco seasoning with refried beans.

2. Assemble layers as follows for each cup:
   - Beans with taco seasoning: 2 tablespoons
   - Sour cream: 2 tablespoons
   - Guacamole: 2 tablespoons
   - Pico de gallo: 2 tablespoons
   - Shredded cheese: 2 tablespoons
   - Tomatoes: 2 teaspoons
   - Scallions and olives: 1 teaspoon

3. Store in refrigerator until ready to serve.

4. Just before serving, garnish each cup with two or three tortilla chips.

PRESSURE COOKER ARTICHOKE AND SPINACH DIP

Spinach and artichoke dip is a classic crowd-pleaser loaded with cheesy goodness.

SERVES 10 | PREP 20 MINS | COOK 4 MINS

INGREDIENTS

3 garlic cloves

1/2 cup vegetable broth

1 (4-ounce) can artichoke hearts, drained

10 ounces frozen spinach

1/2 cup sour cream

8 ounces cream cheese

1/2 cup mayonnaise

1 teaspoon onion powder

16 ounces shredded Parmesan cheese

8 ounces shredded mozzarella

INSTRUCTIONS

1. Place garlic cloves and chicken broth in pressure cooker.

2. Add artichokes, frozen spinach, sour cream, cream cheese, mayonnaise and onion powder to pot.

3. Cook on manual high pressure for 4 minutes.

4. Do a quick release.

5. Stir in Parmesan and mozzarella.

6. Transfer hot dip to bowl.

7. Serve with corn chips or bread bites.

BAKED BRIE WITH BLACKBERRY COMPOTE AND PECANS

Warm cheese, berries and nuts are a heavenly combination that never disappoints.

SERVES 10 | PREP 20 MINS | COOK 35 MINS

INGREDIENTS

1 cup pecan halves

1/2 tablespoon unsalted butter, melted and cooled

1-1/2 tablespoons light brown sugar

2 teaspoons pure maple syrup

1/4 teaspoon ground cinnamon

3/4 teaspoon kosher salt

1/4 teaspoon cayenne pepper

2 cups blackberries, plus more for garnish

1 tablespoon lemon juice, freshly squeezed

1 tablespoon honey

1 teaspoon vanilla extract

1 large wheel Brie, at room temperature

1 handful pomegranate seeds as garnish (optional)

Fresh thyme leaves as garnish (optional)

Crackers for serving

INSTRUCTIONS

1. Preheat oven to 350F.

2. Line baking sheet with parchment paper.

3. Place pecans on sheet and toast for 10 minutes or until fragrant.

4. While nuts are roasting, mix butter, brown sugar, maple syrup, cinnamon, salt and cayenne pepper in bowl.

5. Add pecans to mixture and stir until evenly coated.

6. Spread pecans on baking sheet in single layer and return to oven.

7. Bake for another 10 minutes, stirring every 3 to 4 minutes. Remove from oven and allow to cool.

8. In medium saucepan, heat blackberries, lemon juice, honey and vanilla at medium heat, stirring continuously. As liquid begins to release from berries, turn heat up to medium. Cook, stirring periodically, until mixture is reduced and liquid is syrupy.

9. Line another baking sheet with parchment paper.

10. Carefully slice away top of Brie rind and discard. Leave sides intact. Bake at 350F for 15 minutes or until melted.

11. For plating, top baked Brie with blackberry compote and spicy candied pecans.

12. Garnish with blackberries, pomegranate seeds and fresh thyme leaves.

13. Serve warm with crackers.

VEGAN RAW "CHEESE" SUN-DRIED TOMATO AND PESTO SPREAD

Impress vegans and non-vegans alike with this creamy sun-dried tomato and pesto spread with rice crackers, vegetables or toast on the side.

SERVES 10–12 | PREP 30 MINS | CHILL OVERNIGHT

INGREDIENTS

Vegan cheese

1 cup raw cashews, soaked for 3 hours (not overnight), drained

Juice of 1 lemon

2/3 cups water

2 tablespoons coconut oil

2 teaspoons apple cider vinegar

1/2 teaspoon sea salt

Pesto

1-1/2 cups fresh basil leaves

1/2 cup fresh Italian parsley leaves (stems removed), plus extra for garnish

3 garlic cloves, peeled

1/3 cup pine nuts

1/3 cup raw walnuts

1/4 cup extra-virgin olive oil plus drizzle for garnish

2 teaspoons salt

2/3 cups sun-dried tomatoes, soaked in oil or boiled, and drained

INSTRUCTIONS

1. Line 6-inch baking dish or springform pan with plastic wrap and set aside (greasing will not work).

2. In food processor or high-speed blender, blend cheese ingredients until smooth. Place half of mixture evenly in 6-inch pan.

3. Blend pesto ingredients in food processor or high-speed blender until smooth. Add 1 to 2 tablespoons water if needed for thinning. Add pesto layer on top of cheese mixture, distributing evenly.

4. Cover entire springform pan with wrap or foil and refrigerate overnight. Remove from pan by placing upside down and tapping if needed. Carefully remove plastic and drizzle with touch of olive oil and herbs for garnish.

5. Top with sun-dried tomatoes and layer with remaining cheese.

Find more vegan recipes at thanksgiving.com/tag/vegan

GARLICKY PUMPKIN HUMMUS

Classic hummus gets an autumn upgrade with pumpkin and thyme.

SERVES 6 | PREP 15 MINS | CHILL OVERNIGHT

INGREDIENTS

2 cans (15 ounces each) chickpeas, drained and rinsed

1 can (15 ounces) pumpkin purée

1/4 cup cashew butter

2 tablespoons lemon juice

2 cloves garlic

1-1/2 teaspoons thyme leaves

Kosher salt, to taste

Crackers, pretzels or vegetables

INSTRUCTIONS

1. Add all items to food processor and process until smooth.

2. Taste and season with kosher salt as desired.

3. Place in refrigerator and let sit overnight to let flavors meld.

4. Serve cold with crackers, pretzels or vegetables.

tip / Prep this autumn-inspired hummus the day before to give the flavors time to develop.

HOMEMADE WONTON CRACKERS

These homemade crispy wontons are a healthy alternative to store-bought crackers.

MAKES 50 CRACKERS | PREP 15 MINS | COOK 5 MINS

INGREDIENTS

1/4 cup sesame oil

1/4 cup canola oil

25 wonton wrappers
(1 package)

1/4 cup parsley, minced

Sea salt and pepper to taste

INSTRUCTIONS

1. Line baking tray with parchment paper. Set aside.

2. In small bowl, whisk sesame and canola oils.

3. Place square wonton wrapper on cutting board. Cut square wrappers in half to form rectangles.

4. Lay wonton pieces out in single layer on baking sheet.

5. Brush with oil mixture and lightly sprinkle with parsley, salt and pepper.

6. Bake at 375F for 4 to 5 minutes or until wontons are brown and crispy. Watch carefully: They will burn quickly.

smart swap / Change up the flavors of this recipe by swapping the salt and pepper for paprika, garlic or basil.

TUNA TARTARE

Bright, fresh and flavorful, this tuna tartare is an invigorating contrast to more traditional rich, heavy holiday foods.

SERVES 4–6 | PREP 30 MINS

INGREDIENTS

1 heaping tablespoon fresh ginger, grated

1 teaspoon wasabi powder or paste

2 teaspoons serrano chile, minced

1 cucumber, seeds removed, diced into 1/4-inch pieces

1/4 cup chives, minced

1 lime, zested and juiced

2 teaspoons rice vinegar

1 tablespoon soy sauce

1 tablespoon sesame oil

1 tablespoon Italian parsley, minced

2 tablespoons toasted sesame seeds, plus extra for garnish

1-1/2 pounds sushi-grade tuna steaks, bloodline removed, diced into 1/4-inch pieces

1 teaspoon kosher salt

Several turns of freshly grated black pepper

1 tablespoon black sesame seeds (for garnish)

2 teaspoons chives, minced (for garnish)

INSTRUCTIONS

1. In large bowl, whisk all ingredients except tuna, salt, black pepper, black sesame seeds and chives.

2. Add tuna and stir gently to combine.

3. Spoon tuna tartare onto tops of wonton crackers.

4. Sprinkle with black sesame seeds.

5. Garnish with sprinkle of fresh chives.

6. Keep very cold and serve immediately.

tip / This goes great with our recipe for homemade wonton crackers.

SPICY MINI BACON CHEESEBALLS

Toasted pecans give these dynamite appetizers just a bit of crunch.

MAKES 18 | PREP 30 MINS | CHILL 1 HR

INGREDIENTS

12 ounces cream cheese, softened

1 cup sharp cheddar
cheese, grated

1 teaspoon garlic powder

1 teaspoon smoky paprika

1/2 teaspoon salt

1/4 teaspoon pepper

1 small jalapeño, seeds
removed, finely diced

8 slices cooked bacon, crispy
and finely chopped

1/3 cup fresh chives,
finely chopped

1/2 cup toasted pecans,
finely chopped

18 pretzel sticks

INSTRUCTIONS

1. In large bowl, mix cream cheese, cheddar cheese, garlic powder, paprika, salt, pepper and jalapeno until well blended.

2. Using tablespoon or melon baller, scoop out some cheese and roll into ball. Continue rolling remainder of cheese into similarly sized balls.

3. Arrange all cheese balls on baking sheet lined with parchment paper. Chill in refrigerator for minimum of 1 hour to set.

4. In shallow saucer or bowl, place cooked bacon, chives and pecans. Mix well.

5. Roll each ball into bacon mixture, coating completely on all sides. Place on serving tray.

6. Insert pretzel stick into each ball and serve.

tip / Using a melon baller is a quick and easy way to create uniform cheese balls.

EASY BACON JALAPEÑO CHEESE BALL

This easy bacon jalapeño cheese ball features big bacon and herb flavor, as well as heat from the jalapeño and hot sauce, three tasty cheeses and a crunchy coating of toasted nuts.

SERVES 6–8 | PREP 25 MINS | CHILL OVERNIGHT

INGREDIENTS

8 ounces cream cheese, softened

1/8 teaspoon garlic powder

1/8 teaspoon dried oregano

1 teaspoon dried parsley

1/2 teaspoon hot sauce

1/2 teaspoon Worcestershire sauce

1/2 tablespoon finely minced onions

1-1/2 small jalapeños, minced

2 strips smoked bacon, cooked, diced small

3/4 cup finely shredded pepper jack cheese

1/2 cup finely shredded sharp cheddar cheese

1/2 cup pecans, chopped, toasted

Crackers and vegetables for serving

INSTRUCTIONS

1. Place cream cheese in mixing bowl and beat with handheld mixer until smooth.

2. Mix in garlic powder, dried oregano, dried parsley, hot sauce, Worcestershire sauce, minced onions, jalapeños and bacon.

3. Stir in shredded pepper jack and cheddar cheeses and blend until combined.

4. Taste and adjust seasonings.

5. Form cheese mixture into ball by hand and set aside on plastic wrap.

6. Place toasted chopped pecans on plate. Invert cheese ball onto pecans. Sprinkle pecans all over cheese ball until completely covered, then press nuts into cheese ball to coat evenly.

7. Wrap cheese ball in plastic wrap and refrigerate overnight to allow flavors to blend.

8. Serve cheese ball with crackers and vegetables.

tip / Coat your hands with a little olive oil to keep cheese from sticking when forming the cheese ball.

BEEF MEATBALLS WITH ZESTY CRANBERRY COCKTAIL SAUCE

These delicious meatballs can be kept warm in a slow-cooker, keeping your oven free for the rest of your prep.

MAKES 36 MEATBALLS | PREP 25 MINS | COOK 50-65 MINS

INGREDIENTS

Meatballs

1 pound 80/20 ground beef

1/3 medium onion, finely diced

1 large egg, lightly beaten

1/4 cup whole milk

1/2 teaspoon salt

1/2 teaspoon ground
black pepper

1/2 cup dry breadcrumbs

1-1/2 teaspoons
Worcestershire sauce

2 scallions, green part only,
sliced (optional, for garnish)

Sauce

1 can (12 ounces) jellied
cranberry sauce

1 jar (12 ounces) chili sauce

1 jar (10-1/2 ounces)
red pepper jelly

2 tablespoons brown sugar

1 teaspoon lemon juice

INSTRUCTIONS

1. Preheat oven to 325F. Line baking tray with parchment paper. Arrange wire rack on top of baking tray and spray with cooking spray.

2. In large bowl, mix ground beef, onion, egg, milk, salt, pepper, bread crumbs and Worcestershire sauce by hand until well combined.

3. Roll into firm, tablespoon-sized balls and place on baking sheet lined with wire rack.

4. Bake until meatballs are cooked through, about 20 minutes.

5. In medium bowl, combine cranberry sauce, chili sauce, red pepper jelly, brown sugar and lemon juice and mix well.

6. Place cooked meatballs in slow-cooker on low setting. Pour sauce over top and stir well.

7. Cook until heated (about 30 to 45 minutes).

8. Garnish with sliced scallions, if desired.

tip / If you have leftover cans of cranberry sauce, this is a delicious way to gobble them up.

Free up your oven with more slow-cooker recipes at thanksgiving.com/tag/slow-cooker

TURKEY CRANBERRY MEATBALLS

These nutrient-dense meatballs are roasted to perfection rather than fried.

MAKES 30 MEATBALLS | PREP 25 MINS | COOK 15-20 MINS

INGREDIENTS

2 slices whole-grain seeded bread, toasted

2 cloves garlic

5 Tuscan kale leaves, chopped and stems removed

5 fresh sage leaves

1 pound ground turkey

2 large eggs

1 cup canned cranberry sauce, divided

1/2 teaspoon salt

1/4 teaspoon pepper

INSTRUCTIONS

1. Preheat oven to 400F. Line baking sheet with parchment paper and set aside.

2. In food processor bowl, pulse toast into crumbs. Empty into large bowl. Clean food processor bowl.

3. Add garlic to food processor. Process until chopped.

4. Add kale and sage. Process until roughly chopped. Transfer chopped kale mixture to bowl with breadcrumbs.

5. Stir in ground turkey, eggs and 1/2 cup cranberry sauce.

6. Add salt and pepper; stir until well combined.

7. Shape turkey mixture into 1-inch meatballs.

8. Roast for 15 to 20 minutes, or until internal temperature of meatballs reaches 165F.

9. Serve meatballs hot with toothpicks, along with remaining cranberry sauce on side for dipping.

tip / Use a light touch when shaping the meatballs to prevent toughness.

CARAMELIZED ONION AND SPINACH STUFFED MUSHROOMS

Sweet caramelized onions paired with earthy mushrooms and melted cheese create a beautifully rustic appetizer.

SERVES 10–12 | PREP 20 MINS | COOK 30 MINS　　

INGREDIENTS

1 medium onion, peeled and thinly sliced

1 tablespoon butter

1 teaspoon sugar

3 tablespoons olive oil

8 large Portobello mushrooms, stems removed

1/4 cup finely chopped spinach

Salt and pepper, to taste

1/4 cup freshly grated Parmesan cheese

1/2 cup freshly grated mozzarella cheese

Fresh parsley, for topping (optional)

INSTRUCTIONS

1. Preheat oven to 400F.

2. Rub each mushroom generously with olive oil.

3. In large nonstick skillet over medium heat, add onion slices, butter and sugar. Stir gently and frequently until sweet and caramelized, about 15 minutes.

4. Add finely chopped spinach and sauté for another minute.

5. Stuff mushrooms full with onion and spinach mixture. Season with salt and pepper.

6. Combine Parmesan and mozzarella cheese in small bowl.

7. Top each mushroom evenly with cheese.

8. Bake until golden brown and cheese is melted, about 10 to 14 minutes. If cheese is browning too quickly, cover with foil.

9. Remove, allow to cool slightly and top with fresh parsley.

tip / You can prep these a few hours ahead of time. Just refrigerate until you're ready to bake them.

CHEESY PROSCIUTTO-WRAPPED ASPARAGUS BUNDLES

Parmesan and prosciutto add just a bit of salty heartiness to fresh, bright asparagus. These work well as an appetizer or a side dish.

SERVES 4–6 | PREP 15 MINS | COOK 8 MINS      EF GF GR LC NF Q

INGREDIENTS

6 ounces sliced prosciutto

1/2 pound asparagus, trimmed

1/3 cup shredded Parmesan cheese

1 tablespoon olive oil

INSTRUCTIONS

1. Group trimmed asparagus spears in bundles of three. Wrap one slice of prosciutto around each bundle at an angle, working to cover entire length. Repeat process with remaining prosciutto and asparagus bundles.

2. Heat olive oil in large skillet over medium-high heat.

3. Once oil is hot, add asparagus bundles and cook until prosciutto is crisp and asparagus is tender, about 4 to 5 minutes.

4. Preheat broiler.

5. Transfer asparagus bundles to parchment-lined baking sheet.

6. Pile Parmesan cheese generously on top of bundles.

7. Place baking sheet under broiler for 2 to 3 minutes, watching carefully. Remove from heat as soon as cheese starts to bubble and brown. (The key is to have some of the cheese stay gooey, while some gets crunchy.)

8. Serve immediately.

tip / Is your oven packed with a turkey and sides? You can cook these asparagus bundles in a toaster oven, instead.

CHARCUTERIE BOARD

Impress your guests with a delectable and elegant meat and cheese board you assembled at home.

POSSIBLE INGREDIENTS	TIPS FOR THE PERFECT BOARD
Salami, prosciutto, capicola	1. Offer a variety of contrasting flavors and textures.
Cheddar cheese, blue cheese, Brie cheese	2. Look for complementary flavors and finger-friendly picks.
Pistachios, blueberries, raspberry preserves, Kalamata olives, spicy brown mustard	3. Include a variety of meats, some smoky and others that are zesty, to let your guests create fun and interesting combinations.
	4. Choose at least one cheese that is a familiar standby, like cheddar, and mix it with more adventurous cheeses.
	5. For the perfect contrast, look for some sweet, crunchy, and acidic accompaniments to your board, such as berries, nuts, olives, and capers.
	6. You might also want to add some crackers, pita chips, or sliced baguettes to transport your amazing creations to your mouth.

Soups & Salads

SHREDDED BRUSSELS SPROUTS, APPLE AND WALNUT SALAD

Shred your Brussels sprouts into an amazing side dish accented with crisp apples, toasted walnuts, pomegranate seeds and blue cheese.

SERVES 4-6 | PREP 25 MINS

INGREDIENTS

Salad

1-1/2 pounds Brussels sprouts, shredded

2 small crisp apples, cut into 1/2-inch pieces

1/2 cup walnuts, toasted and chopped

1/3 cup Italian parsley, coarsely chopped

1/4 cup pomegranate seeds

Salt and pepper, to taste

4 ounces blue cheese, crumbled

Vinaigrette (Makes 1 cup)

1/3 cup sherry vinegar

1 shallot, diced

1 tablespoon honey

1 tablespoon Dijon mustard

2/3 cup extra-virgin olive oil

INSTRUCTIONS

1. Toss the Brussels sprouts and apples together in a large bowl.

2. Add the walnuts, parsley and pomegranate seeds.

3. Make vinaigrette by whisking the sherry vinegar, shallots, honey and mustard together. Add extra-virgin olive oil and mix well. Taste and season with salt and pepper. Mix well just before adding to salad.

4. Drizzle about 1/2 cup of vinaigrette over dressing and toss salad well.

5. Sprinkle with blue cheese crumbles.

6. Allow salad to stand a few minutes, or chill in refrigerator no more than two hours before serving.

SMOKY QUINOA BLACK BEAN SALAD

This salad features quinoa, black beans, corn, red peppers and cilantro for some colorful flair.

SERVES 4 | PREP 20 MINS | COOK 20 MINS

INGREDIENTS

1 cup uncooked white quinoa, rinsed

1-3/4 cups cold water

1/4 cup olive oil

1 tablespoon red wine vinegar

1 teaspoon smoked paprika, toasted

1/2 teaspoon ground cumin, toasted

1/4 teaspoon garlic powder

1 teaspoon salt

Freshly cracked black pepper, to taste

1 (15-ounce) can black beans, rinsed, drained

2 red bell peppers, seeded, diced

1-1/2 cups fresh or canned corn, cooked

3 scallions, green and white parts, sliced

2 tablespoons roughly chopped fresh cilantro

INSTRUCTIONS

1. Place the quinoa in a saucepan over high heat. Pour in the water and give the mixture a gentle stir. Place lid on pot and bring the quinoa to a boil. Lower the heat and simmer for 15 minutes or until the quinoa is cooked and the water is absorbed.

2. Turn off the heat and allow the quinoa to rest for 5 minutes. Remove the lid and fluff the quinoa with a fork. Transfer the quinoa to a bowl and refrigerate until cool.

3. In a small bowl, whisk together the olive oil, vinegar, smoked paprika, cumin, garlic powder, salt and freshly cracked black pepper. Set mixture aside.

4. In a large, wide serving dish, arrange the quinoa to cover one half of the dish. In a side-by-side arrangement, place the black beans, red bell peppers and the corn in the dish. Sprinkle the scallions down the middle of the ingredients, separating the quinoa from the others.

5. Drizzle the vinaigrette over the top of the salad.

6. Garnish with chopped cilantro.

7. Serve the salad with extra vinaigrette on the side.

tip / To toast the paprika and cumin, sprinkle them into a small, dry skillet over medium-low heat and shake until the aroma intensifies, then whisk them into the vinaigrette.

RED WINE GRAPE, TANGERINE AND WILD RICE SALAD

Savory wild rice combines with celery, pumpkin seeds, red wine-soaked grapes and tangy orange slices for an unexpected punch of flavor.

SERVES 12 | PREP 20 MINS | COOK 50 MINS PLUS 2 HRS TO ROAST GRAPES

INGREDIENTS

1-1/2 cups wild rice blend

3 cups chicken stock

1 teaspoon salt

1 teaspoon extra-virgin olive oil

4 stalks celery, chopped

1 small red onion, chopped

1-1/2 cups walnuts, toasted

1/2 cup pumpkin seeds, toasted

Roasted grapes

60+ red grapes

1 cup red wine (Merlot or Cabernet Sauvignon)

3/4 cup white sugar

Juice leftover from roasted grapes

2 small cans mandarin oranges, drained

Vinaigrette

1/3 cup balsamic vinegar

Juice from one orange

3/4 cup extra-virgin olive oil

1/2 cup parsley, minced

1/2 cup mint leaves, minced

2 teaspoons basil leaves, minced

Ground pepper to taste

INSTRUCTIONS

Roasted grapes

1. Preheat oven to 200F.

2. Place washed grapes in a damp towel and rub gently to dry.

3. Remove stems from grapes.

4. Place grapes in a shallow casserole dish large enough to spread out the grapes without touching one another.

5. Combine one cup of red wine and 3/4 cup sugar, mix well. Add wine mixture to grapes and stir well.

6. Roast for two hours. Remove from oven and allow to cool. Place in refrigerator with juices for up to two weeks, or use immediately.

Salad

1. Prepare the roasted grapes (directions above).

2. Combine rice, chicken stock, salt and one teaspoon of extra-virgin olive oil in a medium saucepan.

3. Bring to a boil and stir once. Cover with a lid and simmer for 45 minutes or until done. Allow to set covered for 5 minutes

4. Mix together balsamic vinegar, orange juice, 3/4 cup extra-virgin olive oil and red wine juice left over from the roasted grapes.

5. Add herbs and ground pepper to taste. Mix well.

6. To assemble, using a large mixing bowl, place cooked rice blend, celery, onions, nuts, roasted grapes, mandarin oranges and herbs.

7. Five minutes before serving, add the vinaigrette. Mix well. Allow to set for five minutes, then strain off juice. Pour salad into a serving bowl.

8. Serve.

CITRUS, BERRY AND FETA SALAD

This salad is a rainbow-colored feast for the eyes that proves salad doesn't have to be boring.

SERVES 4 | PREP 20 MINS

INGREDIENTS

1 head romaine lettuce, washed and chopped into bite-size pieces

1 blood orange, seeded and sectioned

1/2 cup blueberries

1/2 cup blackberries

1/2 cup raspberries

4 tablespoons crumbled feta cheese

4 tablespoons sliced almonds

1 teaspoon Dijon mustard

1 tablespoon honey

2 tablespoons balsamic vinegar

1/4 cup olive oil

2 tablespoons Meyer lemon juice

Salt and pepper to taste

1 Meyer lemon, peeled and sliced

INSTRUCTIONS

1. Divide romaine lettuce, orange sections, blueberries, blackberries, raspberries, feta cheese and almonds between two plates or bowls.

2. Place mustard, honey, balsamic vinegar, olive oil, lemon juice, salt and pepper into glass cup. Whisk until blended.

3. Just prior to serving, pour vinaigrette over salad.

4. Garnish with lemon slices.

5. Serve.

tip / Out of berries? This salad tastes great with just about any fruit, from apples to grapes, oranges to pineapple.

AUTUMN KALE AND SPINACH SALAD

SERVES 4 | PREP 20 MINS

INGREDIENTS

8 cups baby kale and spinach mix

2 large apples, cubed

1/3 cup crumbled goat cheese

1/3 cup dried cranberries

1/3 cup pumpkin seeds

1/4 cup orange juice

1 tablespoon honey

1 tablespoon pumpkin seed oil

2 teaspoons champagne vinegar

1 clove garlic, minced

Kosher salt and pepper, to taste

INSTRUCTIONS

1. Add kale and spinach mix to a large platter or salad bowl.

2. Top with apples, goat cheese, cranberries and pumpkin seeds.

3. In a medium sized mixing bowl add orange juice, honey, pumpkin seed oil, champagne oil, garlic, salt and pepper.

4. Whisk to fully combine and drizzle over salad.

BEET, APPLE AND ORANGE SALAD

SERVES 4-6 | PREP 15 MINS
COOK 35 MINS

INGREDIENTS

2 Gala apples, cored and chopped

2 oranges, peeled and chopped

4 beets

1 tablespoon white vinegar

1/4 cup plus 2 tablespoons olive oil

2 tablespoons balsamic vinegar

1/2 teaspoon brown sugar

1/4 cup chopped walnuts

INSTRUCTIONS

1. Bring a pot of water and white vinegar to boil.

2. Add the beets to the boiling water and cook for 35 minutes, until tender.

3. Allow the beets to cool to touch, then peel and chop them.

4. Add the beets, apples and oranges to a bowl.

5. In a separate bowl, mix together the olive oil, balsamic vinegar and brown sugar.

6. Add the dressing to the salad and toss well.

7. Sprinkle walnuts on top of the salad when ready to serve.

CELERY ROOT, APPLE AND WALNUT SALAD

SERVES 4 | PREP 18 MINS

INGREDIENTS

1/2 celery root

2 apples

2 tablespoons fresh lemon juice (from 1/2 lemon)

1/4 cup mayonnaise

3/4 teaspoon sugar

Salt

Pepper

1/3 cup walnuts

INSTRUCTIONS

1. Peel and julienne the celery root and apples then immediately mix them with the lemon juice so that they don't turn brown.

2. In a bowl, mix mayonnaise, sugar, salt and pepper. Toss with celery root and apples.

3. Add the walnuts and mix well.

HOLIDAY SALAD WITH ARUGULA AND CRANBERRIES

SERVES 2

INGREDIENTS

1/2 cup plus 1 tablespoon olive oil, divided

2 carrots, chopped

1-1/2 tablespoon red wine vinegar

Salt and pepper to taste

1/2 teaspoon sugar

2 cups arugula

1/4 cup dried cranberries

1/4 cup crumbled goat cheese

2 tablespoons sliced almonds

INSTRUCTIONS

1. In a skillet, cook chopped carrots in one tablespoon olive oil on medium heat, stirring occasionally until tender, about seven minutes.

2. In a medium bowl, whisk together 1/2 cup olive oil, red wine vinegar, salt, pepper and sugar.

3. Toss the arugula with the vinaigrette. Top with dried cranberries, cooked carrots, crumbled goat cheese and sliced almonds.

PEAR SALAD WITH BLOOD ORANGE VINAIGRETTE

This pear salad with blood orange vinaigrette is loaded with fresh flavors and tons of nutrients, making it both tasty and healthy.

SERVES 2 | PREP 20 MINS

INGREDIENTS

Zest of 2 blood oranges

1/4 cup blood orange juice

2 teaspoons sugar

1/4 cup extra-virgin olive oil

4 cups mixed greens (arugula, spinach and radish greens)

1 Bosc pear, skin on and sliced into 1/2-inch pieces

3 blood orange segments

1/4 cup hazelnuts, toasted

1/4 cup goat cheese, crumbled

INSTRUCTIONS

1. In small bowl, whisk blood orange zest, blood orange juice, sugar and olive oil until well blended.

2. In large serving bowl, place mixed greens. Add pear, blood orange segments and hazelnuts.

3. Just before serving, toss vinaigrette into salad and mix well.

4. Top with goat cheese crumbles.

smart swap / Can't find hazelnuts? You can substitute walnuts, pecans or almonds.

CREAMY ONION SOUP WITH BACON NUT CRUMBLE

Toasted walnuts with smoky bacon provide a crunchy contrast to the smoothness of this creamy soup.

SERVES 8 | PREP 25 MINS

INGREDIENTS

5 small potatoes, diced

5 cups chicken broth

6 tablespoons butter

5 large onions, chopped

2/3 cup dry white wine
like Sauvignon Blanc

12 ounces cream cheese,
softened and cut into cubes

3/4 cup milk

2 teaspoons salt

1/2 teaspoon pepper

4 slices bacon

1/2 cup walnuts, toasted

2 tablespoons parsley, minced

INSTRUCTIONS

1. Place the potatoes in a medium saucepan. Add chicken broth. Boil until soft. Once cooked, strain out the potatoes, reserving the cooking liquid. Set aside two cups of liquid. Return the remainder of the liquid to the saucepan.

2. Melt the butter in a skillet, add onions and sauté on low heat for about 20 minutes, or until completely cooked and translucent. Add the white wine. Simmer for another four minutes.

3. Combine the cooked potatoes, cream cheese, sautéed onions with 1-1/2 cups of reserved liquid in a blender, or use an immersion hand blender. Blend well.

4. Pour the soup into the saucepan, along with the remaining liquid, milk, salt and pepper and whisk until well mixed. Simmer on low heat, stirring as needed.

5. Sauté the bacon until crispy. Blot the excess oil off with a paper towel. Crumble bacon into bite-sized pieces. Mix bacon with toasted walnuts and parsley to make the crumble.

6. Pour into individual soup bowls, garnish with toasted nut crumble and serve.

SLOW-COOKER ROASTED GARLIC BAKED POTATO SOUP

Allow guests to sprinkle toppings of their choice onto this decadent soup—it's an interactive dish for kids and adults alike.

SERVES 4-6 | PREP 22 MINS | COOK 4 HRS

INGREDIENTS

3 pounds organic red potatoes

4 cups low-sodium chicken broth

1/4 cup white onion, diced

1 stalk celery, chopped

2 teaspoons Creole seasoning

2 teaspoons black pepper

2 teaspoons garlic powder

2 teaspoons onion powder

1 teaspoon chili powder

1 teaspoon paprika

1/4 cup roasted garlic cloves

1-1/2 cups heavy cream

1 cup Monterey Jack cheese, shredded

1 cup cheddar cheese, shredded

Toppings: green onions, sour cream, cheese

INSTRUCTIONS

1. Rinse potatoes and cut each into four cubes.

2. Place in slow-cooker with broth, onion, celery and spices. Mix well.

3. Cook on high for 3-1/2 hours.

4. Add roasted garlic, cream and cheese.

5. Blend with immersion blender.

6. Cook 30 more minutes, uncovered.

7. Stir and serve with toppings.

VEGAN CAULIFLOWER SOUP

Every bowl of this cauliflower-onion soup is hearty and full-flavored. It's also a great make-ahead option.

SERVES 8 | PREP 20 MINS | COOK 50 MINS

INGREDIENTS

2 tablespoons olive oil

2 sweet white onions, chopped

2 garlic cloves, minced

3 celery stalks, sliced

2 thyme sprigs

1 teaspoon salt

1/4 teaspoon white pepper

1 large head cauliflower, cut into cubes

6 cups vegetable broth

2 tablespoons walnuts, toasted (optional garnish)

2 tablespoons parsley, minced (optional garnish)

INSTRUCTIONS

1. Pour the olive oil in a large Dutch oven or soup pot and warm over low heat.

2. Add the onions, garlic, celery, thyme, salt and white pepper. Heat on medium. Stir and cook until the mixture glistens with oil, then cover the pot and cook, lowering the heat and stirring frequently. Cook for about 20 minutes.

3. Add the cauliflower to the pot and pour in the broth. Bring to a boil.

4. Reduce the heat so the broth simmers gently and cook, uncovered, for another 20 minutes or until the cauliflower is very soft.

5. Puree the soup in batches in a blender, or use an immersion blender, until it is very smooth.

6. Add salt and pepper to taste.

7. Serve garnished with a few toasted walnuts and a pinch of minced parsley.

SLOW-COOKER FRENCH ONION AND SWEET POTATO SOUP

Sweet potatoes add a hearty autumn twist to traditional French onion soup.

SERVES 8 | PREP 25 MINS | COOK 4-10 HRS (DEPENDING ON SLOW-COOKER SETTING)

INGREDIENTS

1/4 cup plus 2 tablespoons butter

4 large yellow onions, thinly sliced

1 tablespoon white sugar

2 large sweet potatoes, peeled and chopped

1 teaspoon minced garlic

7-1/2 cups beef broth

1 teaspoon salt, or to taste

1/4 teaspoon thyme, dried

1/8 teaspoon sage, dried

1 bay leaf

Baguette, sliced for serving

3/4 cup freshly grated mozzarella cheese

1/4 cup freshly grated Parmesan cheese

INSTRUCTIONS

1. Heat the butter in a large pot over medium high heat. Add onions and cook until translucent, about 8 to 10 minutes.

2. Sprinkle sugar over onions and reduce the heat to medium. Cook, stirring occasionally, for ten minutes. Add sweet potatoes and continue to cook until onions begin to turn brown, about another 15 minutes. Add garlic and cook for another minute.

3. Add onion and sweet potato mixture to the slow-cooker. Pour in all the beef broth, salt, thyme, sage and bay leaf.

4. Cook on high for 4 to 6 hours or low for 8 to 10 hours.

5. To serve, pour soup into individual bowls, top each bowl with a slice of the baguette and sprinkle both cheeses evenly over the bread. Broil on high for one to two minutes.

6. Remove from the oven and enjoy.

tip / For more elegant flavor, swap the mozzarella for gouda or Gruyère cheese.

CREAM OF KALE SOUP WITH PARMESAN CRISPS

Wine, cream and leeks are really what make this kale soup irresistible—the kale just gives us a great excuse to have a second serving.

SERVES 10 | PREP 20 MINS | COOK 55 MINS

INGREDIENTS

Soup

2 tablespoons olive oil

1 large leek, cleaned and sliced

2 bunches of lacinato (dinosaur) kale, coarsely chopped

1 cup dry white wine

4 cups vegetable stock

3/4 cup heavy cream

Salt and freshly ground pepper

Parmesan crisps

8 ounces shredded Parmesan cheese

INSTRUCTIONS

1. Heat a large, heavy pot over medium heat. When hot, add the oil, then the leeks and season with salt and pepper.

2. Cook, stirring occasionally, for ten minutes, or until the leeks are soft.

3. Add the chopped kale and stir.

4. Cover and cook for ten minutes.

5. Remove the cover, stir in the wine and stock and bring back to a simmer.

6. Lower the heat a bit and keep at a gentle simmer for about 30 additional minutes, stirring occasionally, until the kale is extremely tender.

7. Remove from the heat and add the cream, stirring to combine.

8. Working in small batches, puree the soup in a blender or food processor.

9. Return the soup to a clean pot and simmer over low heat to warm through.

10. Season to taste with salt and pepper.

11. Line a baking sheet with parchment paper and mist lightly with cooking spray. Heat the oven to 400F.

12. Place large tablespoons of Parmesan cheese on the baking sheet, leaving at least an inch between the piles of cheese.

13. Use your fingers to gently pat down each pile, flattening just a bit to help them cook evenly.

14. Bake for four to five minutes until crisp and golden. Be sure to keep an eye on them in the final minutes so they don't burn.

15. Remove the baking sheet from the oven and allow the crisps to cool for a few minutes before transferring them to a plate.

16. Serve soup in small soup cups with the Parmesan crisps.

Breads

Recipe by Jessica Gavin

HONEY CORNBREAD MUFFINS

These golden muffins have the sweet taste of honey in each bite.

MAKES 12 | PREP 15 MINS | COOK 15 MINS

INGREDIENTS

1 cup yellow cornmeal

1 cup all-purpose flour

1 tablespoon baking powder

1/2 cup granulated sugar

1 teaspoon salt

1 cup reduced-fat or whole milk

2 large eggs

4 tablespoons unsalted butter, melted

1/2 cup honey

3/4 cup yellow corn kernels, cooked (optional)

INSTRUCTIONS

1. Preheat oven to 400F.

2. In a large bowl mix cornmeal, flour, baking powder, sugar and salt.

3. In a medium sized bowl, whisk together milk, eggs, butter and honey.

4. Add the wet ingredients to the dry ingredients and stir until just mixed. Gently fold in the corn.

5. Lightly spray muffin tins with nonstick cooking spray. Skip this step is using paper liners. Fill the muffin tins 2/3 full with the batter.

6. Place the muffin tin on a sheet pan and bake in the center rack of the oven. Bake for 15 minutes, until golden and toothpick inserted in the center, comes out clean.

7. Allow muffins to cool for 5 minutes in the pan, and then transfer to a cooling rack.

ORANGE CRANBERRY MUFFINS

Fresh cranberries add a tasty zip and brighten these baked pastries with their rosy color.

SERVES 12 | PREP 25 MINS | COOK 30 MINS

INGREDIENTS

Streusel

1-1/2 tablespoons brown sugar

1-1/2 tablespoons granulated sugar

1/4 teaspoon orange zest

1/8 teaspoon salt

2 tablespoons butter, melted

6 tablespoons all-purpose flour

Muffins

2 cups all-purpose flour

1 cup granulated sugar

1-1/2 teaspoons baking powder

1/2 teaspoon baking soda

1 teaspoon salt

4 tablespoons butter, cut into chunks

1 large egg

3/4 cup orange juice

1-1/2 cups fresh cranberries, whole or chopped

INSTRUCTIONS

1. Preheat oven to 350F and place muffin papers in muffin pan.

2. For streusel: In a small bowl, stir together the brown sugar, granulated sugar, orange zest, salt and melted butter.

3. Add the flour and stir until the flour creates a paste with the butter and sugars. Set aside.

4. For muffins: In a large mixing bowl, combine the flour, sugar, baking powder, baking soda and salt. Mix well.

5. Add the butter in chunks and mix it into the dry ingredients until the mixture is crumbly.

6. In a small bowl, whisk together the egg and orange juice.

7. Pour the juice mixture into the bowl with the dry ingredients. Stir just until the mixture has moistened. Do not overstir.

8. Add the cranberries and fold them into the batter.

9. Scoop the muffin batter evenly into 12 muffin cups, then top with a generous sprinkle of streusel topping.

10. Bake for 30 minutes, or until the muffins are golden brown on top.

11. Allow the muffins to cool before removing from the pan.

12. Serve.

GRANDMA'S SOUTHERN BUTTERMILK BISCUITS

You haven't had a true Southern biscuit experience until you've made this recipe from scratch: golden, fluffy, buttery and flaky all at the same time.

SERVES 8-10 | PREP 25 MINS | COOK 14 MINS

INGREDIENTS

2 cups all-purpose flour, plus more for work surface

1 tablespoon baking powder

1/2 teaspoon salt

1/2 teaspoon baking soda

1 tablespoon granulated sugar

1/4 cup butter-flavored shortening, cold

3 tablespoons unsalted butter, cold

1 cup buttermilk, cold

1 tablespoon mayonnaise, cold, for brushing

Melted butter, for brushing

tip / Cold ingredients are key! One of the biggest mistakes biscuit-bakers make is using room temperature ingredients.

INSTRUCTIONS

1. Preheat oven to 425F. Line a baking sheet with parchment paper.

2. In a large bowl, sift together flour, baking powder, salt, baking soda and sugar.

3. Cut in butter-flavored shortening with a pastry blender.

4. Grate in butter, tossing occasionally.

5. Stir in buttermilk until dough is wet and sticky.

6. Generously flour the work surface.

7. Turn out the dough onto a lightly floured surface.

8. Sprinkle a small amount of flour on the dough. Gently knead and fold the dough. Add more flour as needed.

9. Fold the dough over several times, creating layers. These layers make the biscuits light and fluffy.

10. Pat the dough into a 1-inch-thick rectangle.

11. Dip the biscuit cutter into flour and cut the biscuits. Do not twist the cutter while cutting the dough.

12. Place biscuits on parchment-lined baking sheet.

13. Brush the tops of the biscuits with a light coating of mayonnaise.

14. Bake for 14 minutes or until the tops of the biscuits are golden. (For a darker golden color, place the biscuits under the broiler for the last 2 minutes.)

15. Remove the biscuits from the oven and brush them with melted butter.

16. Serve warm.

ROSEMARY-MAPLE CORNBREAD MUFFINS

Ditch those traditional rolls and bake these fragrant muffins.

SERVES 12 | PREP 20 MINS | COOK 18 MINS

INGREDIENTS

1 cup cornmeal

1 cup flour

2 teaspoons baking powder

1/4 teaspoon baking soda

3/4 teaspoon salt

2 tablespoons rosemary, finely chopped

3/4 cup whole milk

1/4 cup honey

1/4 cup pure maple syrup

1/2 cup vegetable oil

INSTRUCTIONS

1. Preheat oven to 350F. Spray a muffin pan with nonstick spray and set aside.

2. In a large bowl, whisk together the cornmeal, flour, baking powder, baking soda, salt and chopped rosemary.

3. In another bowl, stir together the milk, honey, maple syrup and vegetable oil.

4. Mix the dry and wet ingredients until just combined. Do not overstir or the muffins will become dense.

5. Fill the prepared muffin pan with the mixture about 3/4 full.

6. Bake 15 to 18 minutes or until golden brown.

BEST BASIC DINNER ROLLS

Nothing is better than warm and flaky homemade rolls right from the oven.

SERVES 12 | PREP 1 HR 10 MINS (INCLUDES RISE TIMES FOR DOUGH) | COOK 20 MINS

INGREDIENTS

2 cups flour

1 package rapid rise yeast

1/2 teaspoon salt

2 tablespoons sugar

1/4 cup water

2 tablespoons butter

1/2 cup milk

INSTRUCTIONS

1. Preheat oven to 375F.

2. Mix together 3/4 cup flour, un-dissolved yeast, salt and sugar. In a saucepan, heat up milk, water and butter until warm, but not boiling.

3. Slowly pour the heated milk mixture into the flour mixture. Beat with an electric mixture for 2 minutes at medium speed. Mix in 1/4 cup flour and beat for 2 more minutes on high. Stir in the remaining flour.

4. Knead on a lightly floured surface until flat, about 8 to 10 minutes. Cover with plastic wrap and allow to rest for 10 minutes.

5. Separate the dough into 12 equal balls. Place in a greased 8-inch round pan. Cover with a towel and allow to rise in a warm place until they double in size, about 30 minutes.

6. Bake 20 minutes or until golden brown.

SWEET POTATO BISCUITS

Light and flaky, these scrumptious homemade sweet potato biscuits come to the holiday table flaunting a fluffy high-rise of golden layers and an enticing rosemary aroma.

SERVES 8 | PREP 25 MINS | COOK 20 MINS

INGREDIENTS

2 to 2-1/2 cups all-purpose flour

1 tablespoon baking powder

1/4 teaspoon baking soda

1 tablespoon granulated sugar

1/2 teaspoon salt

8 tablespoons butter, frozen, grated

1 cup sweet potato (approximately 2 medium), cooked, pureed in a food processor, cold

3/4 cup whole milk, cold

1 teaspoon finely minced fresh rosemary

INSTRUCTIONS

1. Preheat oven to 400F.

2. In a large bowl, combine the flour, baking powder, baking soda, sugar and salt together.

3. Add the frozen grated butter into the flour mixture. Stir just until the butter is coated with the flour mixture.

4. Place sweet potato puree in a large bowl. Add milk and blend until relatively smooth.

5. Add the sweet potato mixture to the flour mixture. Sprinkle with the rosemary. Stir until the ingredients are mixed well and no dry flour is left at the bottom of the bowl.

6. Turn the dough out onto a floured surface and work in just enough extra flour so it doesn't stick to your hands. Be careful not to overwork the dough.

7. With a rolling pin, roll the dough out to about 3/4-inch thickness. Using a biscuit cutter, cut the dough into 8 rounds. Reuse the extra scraps and gently re-roll the dough to make additional biscuits.

8. Line a large baking sheet with parchment paper.

9. Place the biscuits on the parchment-lined baking sheet.

10. Bake for 15 to 20 minutes, or until biscuits are lightly golden brown on top.

11. Serve biscuits warm with softened butter.

tip / Be gentle and quick with the biscuit dough. The best biscuits are made with a light hand.

WHOLE WHEAT DINNER ROLLS WITH PUMPKIN SEEDS

Soft and buttery with just hint of sweetness, these delicious whole wheat dinner rolls with pumpkin seeds are the perfect accompaniment to any holiday meal.

SERVES 12-15 | 4 HR 30 MINS | COOK 15 MINS

INGREDIENTS

1 package dry yeast (2-1/4 teaspoons)

1/2 cup water

2-1/2 tablespoons honey, divided

1 cup milk

2 tablespoons butter

1 tablespoon salt

2-1/2 cups whole wheat flour

2 tablespoons wheat germ

1-1/2 cups all purpose flour (may not use all)

1/3 cup pumpkin seeds

INSTRUCTIONS

1. Place yeast in water and stir. Make certain that the water is 110F when adding yeast. Stir in 1 tablespoon honey.

2. Allow to stand for 8 to 10 minutes, or until the yeast turns bubbly and doubles in volume. Set aside.

3. Then add the remaining 1-1/2 tablespoons of honey, butter and salt with the milk in a small pan. Heat on simmer until the butter melts.

4. Pour the mixture into a large bowl. Be sure to allow it to cool to lukewarm before the next step.

5. Stir yeast mixture into the milk mixture.

6. Add in whole wheat flour and wheat germ, 1/2 cup at a time, while continuously stirring until incorporated.

7. Add enough all-purpose flour to make a soft dough.

8. Turn onto a lightly floured surface and knead several times.

9. Cover with a tea towel and allow to rest in a warm spot until doubled in size, about 1 hour.

10. Place dough back on floured surface. Knead several more times.

11. Divide dough in half. Divide dough again and continue until you have 12 equal portions.

12. Roll each piece of dough into a ball, then place on a parchment-lined baking sheet.

13. Sprinkle pumpkin seeds on top of rolls.

14. Allow to rise again for 2-3 hours, until doubled in size.

15. When ready to bake, preheat oven to 350F.

16. Bake about 15 minutes, until golden in color.

17. Serve warm or at room temperature.

TWISTED ROSEMARY BREADSTICKS

This simple recipe combines puff pastry with melted butter and fresh rosemary and twists it up to make fresh-from-the-oven breadsticks.

SERVES 10 | PREP 10 MINS | COOK 15 MINS

INGREDIENTS

1 package puff pastry (2 sheets)

1 sprig rosemary (roughly 2 tablespoons chopped)

1/4 cup olive oil

Kosher salt

INSTRUCTIONS

1. Preheat oven to 350F.

2. Line 2 heavy large baking sheets with parchment paper.

3. Roughly chop rosemary. In a small bowl, combine chopped rosemary and olive oil.

4. Unfold a puff pastry sheet onto a lightly floured cutting board and roll out into a rectangle approximately 1/8" thick. Using a knife or a pizza cutter, slice the dough into 1-1/2-inch-wide strips.

5. Using a pastry brush, brush the olive oil and rosemary mixture over the cut strips.

6. Separate and twist each strip and transfer to the baking sheet. Repeat with the second sheet of pastry.

7. Sprinkle with kosher salt. Bake for 10 to 15 minutes, until the breadsticks are golden brown. Transfer the breadsticks from the baking sheet to a basket and serve warm.

tip / Sprinkle on some Parmesan cheese for even more flavor.

KETO CAULIFLOWER BREAD

If you've given up carbs to embrace a special diet, your bread craving is going to be satisfied with this no-grain keto cauliflower bread recipe.

MAKES 1 LOAF | PREP 30 MINS | COOK 55 MINS

INGREDIENTS

1 cup prepared cauliflower rice, from one head of cauliflower

2 cups almond flour

1/4 cup psyllium husk

1/2 teaspoon salt

1/2 tsp baking soda

5 eggs, beaten

For decoration

1-1/2 teaspoons pumpkin seeds

1-1/2 teaspoons sesame seeds

1-1/2 teaspoons sunflower seeds

INSTRUCTIONS

1. Preheat oven to 350F.
2. Cut parchment paper into two 3-inch-by-14-inch strips and one 4-inch-by-16-inch strip.
3. Spray nonstick cooking spray on sides and bottom of loaf pan.
4. Line loaf pan with parchment paper: 2 crosswise and 1 lengthwise, spaced evenly apart. Set aside.
5. Prepare cauliflower rice (see instructions below).
6. In large bowl, mix almond flour, psyllium husk, salt and baking soda.
7. Fold in eggs and cauliflower; mix until batter is smooth.
8. Pour batter into pan and smooth with spatula.
9. Sprinkle pumpkin, sesame and sunflower seeds over top.
10. Bake for 55 minutes, until bread is browned on top.
11. Remove from oven and allow to cool before slicing.

Cauliflower Rice

1. Wash and thoroughly dry cauliflower. Remove all greens and cut into 4 equal sections.
2. Use medium-sized holes on box grater (or grater attachment on food processor) to grate cauliflower into rice-like pieces, leaving any large, tough stems behind.
3. Transfer to clean towel or paper towel and press to remove excess moisture (which can make the dish soggy).
4. Sauté cauliflower in large skillet over medium heat in 1 tablespoon olive oil. Cook (but do not brown) until tender, about 5 to 8 minutes.

GLUTEN-FREE CORNBREAD WITH CHERRY BUTTER

Following a gluten-free diet does not mean living a life without your favorite comfort foods—and you're going to love this gluten-free cornbread.

SERVES 4 | PREP 55 MINS | COOK 25 MINS

INGREDIENTS

Cornbread

1 egg

3/4 cup 2% or whole milk

1/3 cup canola oil

1/2 teaspoon salt

1/2 cup granulated sugar

1 tablespoon baking powder

1 cup all-purpose
gluten-free flour

1 cup cornmeal

Cherry butter

1/2 cup fresh cherries, pitted

1/3 cup water

1/3 cup granulated sugar

1/3 cup butter, softened to
room temperature

INSTRUCTIONS

Cornbread

1. Preheat oven to 375F.

2. In a large bowl, whisk together the egg, milk and oil until light and fluffy.

3. Add salt, sugar and baking powder. Mix until combined.

4. Slowly add flour and cornmeal, alternating 1/2 cup at a time. Mix until just combined. Do not overmix.

5. Grease a 9-inch square baking dish.

6. Pour batter into baking dish and bake for 20 to 25 minutes.

Cherry butter

1. In a small pan over medium heat, combine cherries, water and sugar. Simmer until the cherries are soft.

2. Pour cherries into a small colander fitted over a bowl to strain. Transfer cherries to a bowl to cool. Reserve the simple syrup in the bowl for another use.

3. In a food processor, combine butter and cherries. Pulse until well-blended.

4. Place cherry butter in the refrigerator until 30 minutes before serving.

5. Allow cherry butter to come to room temperature.

6. Serve butter with cornbread.

HOMEMADE NO-KNEAD BREAD

This is a simple and savory homemade no-knead sourdough bread that makes a delicious side or starter.

MAKES 1 LOAF | PREP 25 MINS PLUS 22 HOURS FOR RISING | COOK 30 MINS

INGREDIENTS

2 cups bread flour

1 cup whole wheat flour

1-1/2 cups plus 2 tablespoons water, 110F

1 tablespoon honey

1/2 teaspoon active yeast

1 tablespoon dried minced onion

1 tablespoon fresh rosemary, chopped

1 tablespoon unsalted butter

1 teaspoon salt

INSTRUCTIONS

1. In small pan over low heat, melt the butter. When the butter begins to sizzle, add the onion and rosemary. Sauté until the onions begin to brown. Remove the pan from the heat and set aside.

2. Measure the water in a measuring cup and then add the yeast. Set aside.

3. In a large mixing bowl combine the 2 flours. Add the water, yeast and honey and begin to mix. Once a ball begins to form, add the onions, rosemary and salt and mix until all the ingredients are combined. The mixture should resemble really thick pancake batter. Cover the bowl with plastic wrap and set aside to rise for 20 hours.

4. The following day, the dough should have risen and have bubbles just under the surface. Scoop the dough onto a well-floured surface. Liberally sprinkle the top of the dough with more flour. Fold the dough over on itself twice and form a ball. Sprinkle a piece of parchment paper with cornmeal. Place the dough ball seam side down on the paper and cover it loosely with plastic wrap and a clean dish towel. Let the dough rise for 2 hours.

5. A half hour before the dough is ready, preheat oven to 450F and place a baking sheet or baking stone in the oven while it heats. When the dough finishes its second rise, score the top with a sharp knife and transfer the dough on the parchment paper to the baking sheet or stone. Bake for 30 minutes or until the bread becomes golden brown and forms a crunchy crust.

CORNUCOPIA BREAD BASKET

The cornucopia, or horn of plenty, symbolizes all the bounty we're thankful for. This edible version doubles as a centerpiece.

INGREDIENTS

Large water bottle (the larger the bottle, the larger the cornucopia to fill!)

Aluminum foil

Nonstick cooking spray

Ready-made dough, such as pizza dough. (Crescent or biscuit dough is too flaky)

Butter

INSTRUCTIONS

1. Wrap the bottle with several layers of foil, which will provide support for the dough. Shape it into the familiar cornucopia horn and curl the tail to create the traditional look.

2. Coat foil mold liberally on all sides with nonstick cooking spray.

3. Preheat oven to 350F.

4. Flour cutting board and roll dough into a rectangle. Using a pizza cutter, slice dough into 1-inch-wide strips.

5. Lay strips along foil mold, starting at the wide opening end. Overlap strips slightly and don't leave any gaps. Leave an inch or so at the top for something to hold onto. As the dough warms and settles a bit, you may need to go back and straighten some sections out or overlap them again. Continue until you have covered the whole horn.

6. Add a fancy braid to the opening of the cornucopia by laying three strips of dough on cutting board, pinch them together at the top, and braid them. Pinch the other end together and wrap your braid around the mouth of the horn, hiding the seam on the underside. Leave a little space at the top for a foil edge to grasp to remove the mold after baking.

7. Remove plastic bottle from the mold. Brush cornucopia with melted butter and bake for 25 to 30 minutes on the lower rack, or until it turns a golden, shiny brown. If it starts to get a little too brown, cover the darkening area with a sheet of foil.

8. Remove from the oven, allow the horn to cool fully, and then gently remove your foil mold.

9. Fill your horn with delicious, colorful items like fresh fruits, vegetables, gourds, nuts, bread rolls or treats such as cookies or muffins.

Sides

MAPLE BROWN BUTTER MASHED SWEET POTATOES

Rich with brown butter, naturally sweetened and topped with chopped pecans, this is the holiday recipe your family will be talking about long after the holidays.

SERVES 8-10 | PREP 25 MINS | COOK 10 MINS

INGREDIENTS

3 pounds sweet potatoes, peeled, diced

6 tablespoons unsalted butter, cut into 12 pieces

1/4 cup real maple syrup

1/4 teaspoon ground cinnamon

1/8 teaspoon freshly grated nutmeg

1/8 teaspoon ground cloves

1/4 cup chopped pecans

INSTRUCTIONS

1. Add the sweet potatoes to a large pot and cover with cold water. Place a lid on the pot and bring the water to a boil over high heat. Reduce the heat to a simmer and cook the potatoes for 5 to 10 minutes or until they are tender when pierced with a fork.

2. Drain the sweet potatoes into a colander.

3. Place the sweet potatoes in a large bowl and use a potato masher to mash them until smooth, leaving a few chunks. Set aside.

4. Place the butter in a skillet over medium-low heat. Melt the butter until it begins to foam. Continue to cook the butter, stirring constantly, until the butter solids begin to brown. Watch the butter closely and immediately remove it from the heat when it reaches a deep brown color and smells nutty or caramel-like.

5. Immediately pour the browned butter into a separate bowl to stop the cooking process.

6. Whisk the maple syrup into the butter.

7. Pour the butter mixture into the mashed sweet potatoes, reserving 1 to 2 tablespoons of the maple brown butter to drizzle over the top as a garnish.

8. Add the cinnamon, nutmeg and cloves to the mashed sweet potatoes, stirring to combine.

9. Taste the sweet potatoes and adjust the syrup, spices, or salt, if needed.

10. Sprinkle the chopped pecans over the top of the sweet potatoes.

11. Drizzle the mashed sweet potatoes with the remaining maple brown butter just before serving.

12. Serve hot.

HONEY CINNAMON SWEET POTATOES

Offer guests some side dish variety by serving roasted chunks of buttery sweet potatoes alongside more traditional mashed potatoes.

SERVES 4 | PREP 20 MINS | COOK 30 MINS

INGREDIENTS

3 tablespoons melted butter

2 tablespoons honey

3 to 4 heavy dashes ground cinnamon

20 ounces sweet potatoes, peeled, cut into bite-sized pieces

INSTRUCTIONS

1. Preheat oven to 375F.

2. In a large bowl, whisk together melted butter, honey and ground cinnamon.

3. Add sweet potatoes and stir until coated with butter mixture.

4. Line a baking sheet with parchment paper.

5. Spread sweet potatoes evenly on the baking tray in a single layer.

6. Roast for 30 minutes or until sweet potatoes are fork-tender.

7. Transfer sweet potatoes to a serving platter. Drizzle with extra honey, if desired.

8. Serve hot.

SOUR CREAM, CHEDDAR AND CHIVE MASHED POTATOES

If your regular holiday mashed potatoes need a cheesy makeover, this can be your new go-to.

SERVES 6 | PREP 20 MINS | COOK 1 HR

INGREDIENTS

2 pounds Yukon gold potatoes, washed and cut into 3-inch pieces

6 cups chicken broth

6 tablespoons butter, sliced into small cubes (at room temperature)

3/4 cup sour cream

1/3 cup half-and-half

2 cups sharp cheddar cheese, divided

2 tablespoons fresh chives, thinly sliced

2 tablespoons butter, melted

Salt and pepper

INSTRUCTIONS

1. Preheat oven to 350F.
2. Place potatoes in large pot and cover with chicken broth. Bring to boil. Cover and reduce heat to medium.
3. Simmer until potatoes are fork-tender and some are falling apart, 20 to 30 minutes.
4. Drain potatoes.
5. Add butter.
6. Once butter has melted, mash with potato masher.
7. Gently fold in sour cream and half-and-half.
8. Stir in 1 cup shredded cheddar cheese and chives until just combined.
9. Taste and season with salt and pepper.
10. Gently mash potatoes again until all large lumps are gone and potatoes are smooth.
11. Using melted butter, grease 9-by-9-inch casserole dish. Set aside.
12. Pour half of potatoes into prepared pan and sprinkle with a layer of cheese (approximately 1/2 cup).
13. Top with remaining potatoes and finish with final layer of cheddar cheese (another 1/2 cup).
14. Cover loosely with aluminum foil and bake for 20 to 30 minutes, or until cheese is melted.
15. Remove foil. Garnish with fresh chives.

tip / Sprinkle with crumbled bacon and chives to add color, texture and flavor.

CHUNKY MASHED POTATOES

An updated take on classic mashed potatoes, this side dish provides all the potato creaminess you love with a fresh, chunky texture.

SERVES 6-8 | PREP 20 MINS | COOK 15 MINS   (EF) (GF) (GR) (NF) (V)

INGREDIENTS

3 pounds red-skinned potatoes

2 tablespoons butter

2/3 cup sour cream

1 clove garlic, minced

4 whole green onions, sliced

Salt and freshly ground
black pepper, to taste

INSTRUCTIONS

1. Scrub potatoes under running water, removing dirt. Do not peel.

2. Cut potatoes into 1-inch cubes.

3. Place diced potatoes in a large pot and cover with cold water.

4. Set pot over high heat and bring water to a boil. Boil for 15 minutes or until potatoes are tender when pierced with a fork.

5. Drain potatoes in a colander and return them to the pot.

6. Add butter, sour cream, garlic, green onions, salt and freshly ground black pepper.

7. With a potato masher, mash ingredients together. Taste potatoes and adjust seasoning.

8. Cover pot and keep warm until ready to serve.

tip / Sprinkle with chives for an added touch of flavor.

SLOW-COOKER MILLION-DOLLAR MASHED POTATOES

These potatoes owe their name to the rich, flavorful texture provided by butter and cream cheese, mashed to perfection with chicken broth and milk.

SERVES 8-10 | PREP 25 MINS | COOK 4-5 HRS

INGREDIENTS

5 pounds russet potatoes, peeled and cut into 1-inch chunks

1 cup (2 sticks) salted butter, cut into cubes, divided

1 (32-ounce) carton chicken broth

1 (8-ounce) package cream cheese, softened, cut into cubes

1/4 cup whole milk or more, to taste

Salt and freshly ground black pepper to taste

2 tablespoons minced Italian parsley

INSTRUCTIONS

1. Place the potatoes into the bottom of a 6-quart slow-cooker.

2. Dot potatoes with half the cubed butter.

3. Pour chicken broth over potatoes.

4. Cover and cook on high for 4 to 5 hours. Potatoes are ready when they are fork-tender.

5. Carefully drain excess broth from cooked potatoes.

6. Place potatoes back into the slow-cooker.

7. Add in remaining stick of cubed butter, cream cheese and milk. Season with salt and pepper to taste.

8. Mash the potatoes with a potato masher until smooth. Add more milk if needed.

9. Cover and keep the mashed potatoes on the warm setting until ready to serve.

10. Just before serving, garnish with minced parsley.

tip / You can keep these warm in the slow-cooker until holiday table showtime.

SCALLOPED POTATOES

Potatoes simmered in cream sauce are generously topped with shredded Gouda and cheddar cheeses that brown and bubble as the casserole bakes to perfection.

SERVES 8 | PREP 25 MINS | COOK 1 HR 24 MIN

INGREDIENTS

2 tablespoons unsalted butter

2 shallots, diced

2 cups heavy cream

2 cups whole milk

1 teaspoon fresh or dried thyme, plus extra for garnish

1/4 teaspoon ground nutmeg

Salt to taste

Freshly ground black pepper to taste

4 pounds russet potatoes, peeled, thinly sliced

8 ounces smoked Gouda cheese, shredded

8 ounces cheddar cheese, shredded

INSTRUCTIONS

1. Preheat oven to 375F.

2. In a large pot over medium heat, melt the butter and cook the shallots, stirring often, until softened.

3. Add the cream, milk, thyme and nutmeg. Season with salt and pepper, stir and bring the mixture to a simmer.

4. Add the potatoes and cook on low heat with lid slightly ajar, until tender, 30 to 35 minutes. Stir occasionally. Be careful not to allow mixture to cook too fast and stick.

5. Coat a large baking dish with nonstick cooking spray.

6. Pour the potato mixture into the baking dish. Top with the shredded cheeses.

7. Bake for 20 to 25 minutes or until the top is slightly golden.

8. Place the scalloped potatoes under the broiler for 3 to 4 minutes to caramelize the cheese.

9. Remove and let the potatoes rest for at least 15 minutes.

10. Sprinkle with extra thyme as a garnish.

11. Serve warm.

CAULIFLOWER MASHED POTATOES WITH SWISS CHARD

This recipe blends potatoes with cauliflower and Swiss chard for a lighter version of the typical mashed potato dish.

SERVES 4 | PREP 25 MINS | COOK 25 MINS

INGREDIENTS

2-1/2 teaspoons salt, divided

3 cups cauliflower, cut into florets

1 pound white potatoes, peeled, cut into 2-inch cubes

1/4 cup heavy cream

4 tablespoons butter, divided

1 1/2 teaspoons salt

3 cloves garlic, minced

1 leek, thinly sliced, white part only

2 cups Swiss chard leaves, ribs removed, cut into 1-inch pieces

Freshly ground black pepper, to taste

INSTRUCTIONS

1. In a medium-sized stockpot over high heat, combine 2 quarts water and 1 teaspoon salt. Bring to a boil.

2. Add cauliflower and potatoes. Reduce the heat to medium-low and cook uncovered for 15 to 17 minutes or until the vegetables are very tender.

3. In a small saucepan over medium heat, add cream, 2 tablespoons butter and 1-1/2 teaspoons salt. Whisk until the butter is melted and the mixture is smooth.

4. In a large skillet over medium heat, melt the remaining 2 tablespoons butter. Add garlic and leeks and cook, stirring often, for 5 minutes or until they are tender, aromatic and lightly browned.

5. Add Swiss chard to the garlic mixture and cook, stirring often, for 2 minutes. Season to taste with salt and pepper. Remove from heat and set aside.

6. Drain the water from the cauliflower and potatoes. Return them to the empty dry pot. Use a potato masher to lightly mash the mixture.

7. Slowly add the warmed cream mixture to the lightly mashed cauliflower and potatoes and continue to mash.

8. Adjust the seasonings with more salt and pepper, if needed, to taste.

9. Stir the chard mixture into the mashed cauliflower and potatoes.

10. Serve warm.

ROASTED POBLANO CREAMED CORN

This recipe brings a bit of the Southwest to your holiday table. And if you're looking for more kick, add a bigger dash of cayenne pepper.

SERVES 8 | PREP 20 MINS | COOK 22-25 MINS

INGREDIENTS

3 tablespoons olive oil, divided 1 tablespoon and 2 tablespoons

3 poblano peppers, washed and dried

4-5 green onions, ends trimmed, cut into small pieces

8 ears corn, cleaned, kernels cut off the cob

2/3 cup water

1/2 teaspoon salt

1/4 teaspoon ground black pepper

1/4 teaspoon cayenne pepper

1/2 cup heavy cream

INSTRUCTIONS

1. Preheat the grill to medium-high heat. Drizzle 1 tablespoon olive oil over the poblano peppers. When hot, add the peppers to the grill. Cook, turning once or twice, until blacked on all sides, or 6 to 8 minutes.

2. Remove from the grill and place them in a deep bowl covered in plastic wrap. (This will help steam the pepper to loosen the skins.)

3. When cool to the touch, remove the skin from the peppers. Cut off the top and remove the seeds. Dice the peppers and set aside.

4. Add the remaining 2 tablespoons of olive oil to a skillet over medium heat. When hot, add the green onion and cook for 2 to 3 minutes, or until they soften.

5. Add the corn kernels, the poblano pieces and water to the skillet. Season with salt, black pepper and cayenne pepper.

6. Bring the mixture to a boil, then reduce the heat to simmer. Cover the skillet and simmer for 5 to 8 minutes, or until the corn is tender.

7. Add the heavy cream to the mixture. Stir and cook uncovered on low heat, until the cream thickens.

8. Transfer to a serving dish.

BALSAMIC AND PARMESAN ROASTED CAULIFLOWER

With a subtly nutty flavor accented with balsamic vinegar and Parmesan cheese, this recipe couldn't be any easier to prepare.

SERVES 6 | PREP 15 MINS | COOK 30 MINS

INGREDIENTS

8 cups cauliflower florets (about 1 large head)

2 tablespoons extra-virgin olive oil

1 teaspoon dried marjoram

1/4 teaspoon salt

Freshly ground pepper

2 tablespoons balsamic vinegar

1/2 cup finely shredded Parmesan cheese

INSTRUCTIONS

1. Preheat oven to 450F.

2. Cut cauliflower into 1-inch-thick slices.

3. In large bowl, toss cauliflower, oil, marjoram, salt and pepper.

4. Spread cauliflower on large, rimmed baking sheet lined with parchment paper. Roast until it begins to soften and brown on bottom, 15 to 20 minutes.

5. Toss cauliflower with balsamic vinegar and sprinkle with cheese.

6. Return pan to oven and roast until cheese is melted and moisture has evaporated, approximately 5 to 10 minutes.

Recipe by Jessica Gavin

GREEN BEANS WITH CRUNCHY ALMONDS

This quick side dish elevates traditional green bean recipes with the flavors of orange, onion and almonds.

SERVES 4 | PREP 10 MINS | COOK 10 MINS

INGREDIENTS

4 quarts water, divided

1-1/8 teaspoon kosher salt, divided

4 cups ice cubes

1 pound green beans or haricot verts

1 tablespoon olive oil

3/4 cup red onions, thinly sliced

2 cloves garlic, thinly sliced

1 teaspoon orange rind, grated

2 tablespoons orange juice

1/8 teaspoon black pepper

1 tablespoon sliced almonds

INSTRUCTIONS

1. Add 3 quarts of water and 1 teaspoon salt to a large pot. Heat pot over high heat until a rolling boil is reached and large bubbles break the surface.

2. Add green beans to boiling water and cook for 2 minutes.

3. Drain and transfer to a large bowl filled with ice water. Allow beans to sit in ice bath for at least 5 minutes, and then drain well.

4. Heat a large skillet over medium-high heat. Add oil to the pan, swirl to coat.

5. Add red onions and garlic, sauté 3 minutes or until tender, do not allow garlic to brown.

6. Add green beans to the pan and stir well.

7. Add orange rind and juice, 1/8 teaspoon salt and pepper, sauté 2 minutes. Season with more salt and pepper as desired.

8. Serve beans warm topped with almonds.

PRESSURE COOKER GREEN BEAN CASSEROLE

With two kinds of cheese and a rich mushroom soup, this casserole is as gooey and rich as they come.

SERVES 8 | PREP 20 MINS | COOK 20 MINS

INGREDIENTS

1 tablespoon flour

2 tablespoons water

2 teaspoons olive oil

3 garlic cloves, minced

5 cups fresh green beans, stems removed

1 can cream of mushroom soup

1/2 cup mozzarella cheese, shredded

1 cup sharp cheddar cheese, shredded

1 cup mozzarella cheese, cut into small cubes

1/3 cup panko breadcrumbs

1-1/2 cup french-fried onions

1/2 teaspoon salt

1/4 teaspoon pepper

INSTRUCTIONS

1. In small bowl, combine flour and water to create slurry.

2. Turn pressure cooker to sauté setting.

3. Add olive oil and garlic. Cook for 1 to 2 minutes.

4. Add cream of mushroom soup and green beans.

5. Stir in salt and pepper.

6. Place lid on pot and seal.

7. Cook on manual high-pressure setting for 12 minutes.

8. When pressure cooker beeps to indicate cooking cycle is complete, use proper procedure for the quick-release steam valve.

9. Turn pressure cooker to sauté.

10. Add slurry to pot.

11. Add 1/2 cup cheddar cheese and 1/4 cup shredded mozzarella.

12. Stir and allow to sauté until cheese has melted.

13. Preheat oven to 425F.

14. Spray large casserole dish with nonstick cooking spray.

15. Pour mixture into large casserole dish.

16. Mix mozzarella cubes throughout casserole.

17. Top with remaining shredded cheese, panko breadcrumbs and fried onions.

18. Bake for 5 to 7 minutes.

GLUTEN-FREE, PALEO & VEGAN GREEN BEAN CASSEROLE

This is just like the classic green bean casserole only it's been reworked into a homemade recipe for those eating vegan, gluten-free and paleo diets.

SERVES 6 | PREP 20 MINS, PLUS 8 HRS TO OVERNIGHT TO SOAK CASHEWS | COOK 25 MINS

INGREDIENTS

1 cup raw cashews

3 large shallots, sliced 1/8-inch thick

1/4 cup almond meal or flour

1 tablespoon arrowroot flour (or cornstarch)

1/2 teaspoon fresh ground pepper

1/2 teaspoon sea salt

7 tablespoons olive oil, divided

10 ounces brown or white button mushrooms, sliced

1 medium onion, chopped

6 medium cloves of garlic, minced or pressed

1- 1/2 pounds fresh green beans, tips snipped off

3 sprigs fresh thyme

1 fresh bay leaf or 2 dry bay leaves

1 cup vegetable stock

Salt and freshly ground pepper to taste

INSTRUCTIONS

1. Place the cashews in a medium-sized bowl and completely submerge under water. Cover with plastic wrap and refrigerate for 8 hours or overnight. Once the cashews have soaked, drain them and rinse thoroughly.

2. Place the cashews in a blender or food processor and add 1/2 cup water. Process on high speed until pureed into a thick cream consistency.

3. In a medium bowl, mix almond meal, arrowroot flour, ground pepper and salt. Add in sliced shallots and toss to evenly coat. Heat 3 tablespoons of oil in a large sauté pan or skillet on high heat. Once the oil starts to shimmer (but before it starts to smoke) reduce the heat slightly to medium-high, add the coated shallots and fry, stirring constantly, until they are golden brown, about 5 minutes. Once golden brown, move them to a baking sheet lined with a double layer of paper towels.

4. Add 2 more tablespoons of oil to the sauté pan or skillet and turn to medium heat. Add the sliced mushrooms and cook, stirring frequently, until they are brown, about 5 to 7 minutes. Pour the mushrooms and any accumulated liquid into a heatproof bowl.

5. Add the final 2 tablespoons of oil to the sauté pan or skillet and turn the heat to medium. Add the chopped onion and cook until soft, about 2 to 3 minutes. Add the garlic and cook until fragrant, about 30 seconds.

6. Add the green beans, thyme, bay leaves, pureed cashews and vegetable stock. Cook, stirring frequently, until the beans are al dente, about 5 minutes.

7. Add mushrooms and liquid and continue to cook for another 5 minutes, or until the green beans are tender and the sauce has thickened.

8. Once done, season with salt and pepper to taste. Remove the thyme and bay leaves before plating and sprinkle with fried shallots before serving.

VEGAN GREEN BEAN CASSEROLE

There's nothing quite like a warm casserole on your holiday table, so wow your guests with this savory vegan green bean casserole.

SERVES 4-6 | PREP 20 MINS | COOK 38 MINS

INGREDIENTS

2 tablespoons sea salt

1 pound fresh green beans, rinsed, trimmed and cut in half

2 tablespoons vegan butter or olive oil

1 shallot, minced

2 cloves garlic, minced

1 teaspoon salt

1/2 teaspoon pepper

1 cup mushrooms (button, baby bella, or cremini), finely chopped

2 tablespoons all-purpose flour

3/4 cup vegetable stock

1 cup unsweetened plain almond milk

1-1/2 cups vegan french-fried onions, divided

Find more vegan recipes at thanksgiving.com/tag/vegan

INSTRUCTIONS

1. Preheat oven to 400F.

2. Bring a large pot of water to a boil and add 2 tablespoons salt.

3. Add green beans and cook for 5 minutes, then drain and place in an ice water bath to stop cooking. Drain and set aside.

4. In a large oven-safe skillet over medium heat, add vegan butter or olive oil and heat for 2 to 3 minutes.

5. Add shallots and garlic. Season with salt and pepper and stir. Cook for 2 to 3 minutes, then add mushrooms and cook for 4 minutes more or until lightly browned.

6. Sprinkle in flour and whisk to stir, coating the vegetables. Cook for 1 minute, then slowly add in vegetable stock, whisking well to incorporate.

7. Add almond milk and whisk again. Reduce heat to low to thicken. Cook for 5 to 7 minutes more, until thick and bubbly.

8. Add 1/2 the onions to the sauce.

9. Place green beans in a casserole dish. Pour sauce over the beans and toss. Top with remaining onions.

10. Bake for 15 minutes, or until warmed through, bubbly and slightly browned on top.

SOUTHERN GREEN BEANS WITH ROASTED GARLIC

Dig into this dish of tender green beans and smoky chunks of ham intensely flavored with an entire head of roasted garlic.

SERVES 4 | PREP 20 MINS | COOK 1 HR 9 MINS

INGREDIENTS

2 tablespoons butter

1/2 of a whole white onion, diced

1 whole head of garlic, roasted, chopped, divided

1 cup diced smoked ham

2 cups chicken broth

1 teaspoon red pepper flakes

1 teaspoon salt

1/2 teaspoon freshly ground black pepper

1-1/2 pounds fresh green beans, ends removed, left whole

INSTRUCTIONS

1. In a large pan over medium-high heat, melt the butter.

2. Add the onion, 5 cloves of roasted garlic and smoked ham. Cook, stirring often, for 3 to 4 minutes.

3. Pour in the chicken broth and bring the mixture to a boil.

4. Stir in the red pepper flakes, salt and pepper.

5. Add the green beans to the pot. Reduce the heat to medium-low and cover the pot with a lid. Simmer for 1 hour.

6. Remove the pot from the heat and add the remainder of the whole roasted garlic cloves, stirring to combine.

7. Use a slotted spoon to transfer the green bean mixture to a serving dish. Serve hot.

Recipe by Monique Kilgore

CREAMY BAKED MACARONI AND CHEESE

This simple baked macaroni and cheese recipe features just two cheeses, but delivers incredible cheesy flavor that's a crowd-pleaser.

SERVES 6-8 | PREP 30 MINS | COOK 30 MINS

INGREDIENTS

3 cups elbow macaroni, uncooked

Salt, pepper and garlic powder to taste

2 tablespoons butter

2 tablespoons flour

1 cup half and half (warmed)

3 1/2 cups colby Jack cheese, shredded and divided

1/2 cup smoked cheddar cheese, shredded and divided

1 1/2 cups whole milk

2 eggs, slightly beaten

Salt and pepper

INSTRUCTIONS

1. Preheat oven to 350F.

2. Butter an 8x10 casserole dish. Set aside.

3. Bring a large pot of seasoned water (salt, pepper, garlic powder) to a boil.

4. Cook pasta until a little under al dente, about 7 minutes. Drain and set aside.

5. In a large saucepan, over medium heat, melt butter.

6. Whisk in flour and continue stirring until golden.

7. Slowly whisk in half and half. Continue stirring until smooth.

8. Stir in 1 cup colby Jack cheese until sauce is creamy.

9. Pour cheese sauce over macaroni, tossing to coat.

10. Pour macaroni into prepared pan. Set aside.

11. In a large bowl, add milk, 2 cups colby Jack cheese, and 1/4 cup smoked cheddar.

12. Add salt and pepper to taste.

13. Add in eggs and stir well.

14. Pour egg mixture over the macaroni. Use a spatula to help push the mixture throughout.

15. Sprinkle the top with remaining cheeses. You may not need all of it.

16. Bake for 25 minutes and check. Bake for up to 10 more minutes.

17. Let sit for 10 minutes before serving.

PRESSURE COOKER MAC AND CHEESE

This classic side dish is so creamy and rich, your guests will never believe it came out of your pressure cooker.

SERVES 6-8 | PREP 10 MINS | COOK 6 MINS

INGREDIENTS

1 pound elbow macaroni

4 tablespoons butter

4 cups water

2 teaspoons dry ground mustard

2 teaspoons kosher or sea salt

1/2 teaspoon black pepper

1 cup evaporated milk

8 ounces sharp cheddar cheese

8 ounces Monterey jack cheese

1/2 cup Parmesan cheese

INSTRUCTIONS

1. Add macaroni, butter, water, mustard, salt and pepper to pressure cooker.

2. Secure the lid, select manual and high pressure for four minutes. (Note: if the directions on your boxed macaroni have a boil time that is less than six minutes, cook on high pressure for only three minutes).

3. Once complete, use a quick release to release the pressure. Open lid and check that the pasta is cooked completely. If not, select sauté and cook for another two minutes until pasta is cooked.

4. Add in evaporated milk and each of the cheeses. Continue to mix and stir until creamy. Add any extra salt to taste.

5. Serve hot.

KETO STUFFING

This recipe keep carbs at bay while still providing great flavor and texture.

SERVES 4 | PREP 15 MINS | COOK 30 MINS

INGREDIENTS

4 slices keto bread (or rolls) crumbled

2 tablespoons olive oil, divided

3 tablespoons butter

2 stalks celery, roughly chopped

1/4 cup leeks, sliced

1/2 teaspoons garlic, minced

1 teaspoon Italian blend seasoning, or 1 tablespoon each fresh parsley, thyme and oregano (all minced)

1/4 teaspoon fresh sage, minced

1/2 teaspoon each salt and pepper

1/2 teaspoon celery salt (optional)

3/4 cup chicken broth

INSTRUCTIONS

1. Preheat oven to 350F.
2. Place keto bread into a large cast-iron skillet or casserole dish.
3. Drizzle with 1 tablespoon olive oil and bake for about 5 minutes until lightly browned.
4. Place toasted breadcrumble in bowl; set aside.
5. Wipe skillet with paper towel. Place skillet on burner, add butter and 1 tablespoon olive oil and melt.
6. Add celery, leeks, garlic, seasoning blend, sage, salt and pepper. Sauté chopped vegetables for 3–5 minutes.
7. Add toasted breadcrumbs to skillet.
8. Slowly add chicken broth 1/4 cup at a time to skillet, stirring continuously.
9. Cover skillet with foil.
10. Place skillet in oven.
11. Bake covered for 10 to 15 minutes.
12. Remove foil. Bake an additional 5 minutes.
13. Serve.

Find more keto recipes at
thanksgiving.com/tag/keto

GRAIN-FREE STUFFING

Craving a holiday stuffing that's good for you? Try our robust grain-free stuffing.

SERVES 4 | PREP 20 MINS | COOK 45 MINS

INGREDIENTS

4 cups parsnips, cut into 1/2-inch chunks

1 cup carrots, cut into 1/2-inch chunks

1 cup roughly chopped yellow onion

1 tablespoon coconut oil

4 garlic cloves, minced

1/2 cup walnuts, toasted

10 ounces mushrooms, roughly chopped

1-1/2 teaspoons fresh thyme leaves

12 leaves fresh sage, minced

Salt and freshly ground black pepper, to taste

1 tablespoon olive oil

INSTRUCTIONS

1. Preheat oven to 400F.

2. Line 2 baking sheets with parchment paper.

3. Arrange the chopped parsnips and carrots in a single layer on one of the lined baking sheets. Arrange the chopped onions in a single layer on the second lined baking sheet.

4. Roast both pans of vegetables for 15 minutes. Use a spatula to stir the vegetables, making sure they cook evenly and don't burn. Continue to roast for 15 minutes or until the vegetables are tender. Watch the onions and if they cook faster than the carrots and parsnips, remove them from the oven and set aside.

5. Melt the coconut oil in a medium-sized skillet over medium heat. Add the garlic and cook, stirring often, for 5 minutes.

6. Add the walnuts and mushrooms and cook, stirring often, for 8 to 10 minutes or until the mushrooms are tender.

7. In a large bowl, combine the roasted vegetables, mushroom mixture, thyme and sage. Season with salt and pepper.

8. Drizzle the stuffing with olive oil. Serve hot.

GRUYÈRE, HAM AND ONION STUFFING

This ham, Gruyère and onion stuffing may sound complicated but is easy to make and packed with flavor.

SERVES 12 | PREP 20 MINS | COOK 1 HR 5 MINS

INGREDIENTS

1-1/2 cups chicken stock

2 eggs

16 to 20 ounces sourdough bread cubes, lightly toasted

1 tablespoon olive oil

2 whole small onions, diced

1 cup diced cooked ham

2 ounces Gruyère cheese, diced

1/4 cup fresh flat-leaf parsley, roughly chopped

INSTRUCTIONS

1. Preheat oven to 350F. Spray nonstick cooking spray on a casserole dish large enough to hold the cubes of bread. Set aside.

2. In a large bowl, whisk together the chicken stock and eggs.

3. Add the toasted sourdough bread cubes to egg mixture and toss until well-combined.

4. In a large skillet over medium-high heat, add olive oil and swirl to coat the bottom of the skillet.

5. Add onions and sauté for 5 minutes.

6. Add bread cubes and ham to the onions.

7. Reduce heat to low and cook, stirring often, for 20 minutes.

8. Remove the skillet from the heat and stir the Gruyère cheese and parsley into the bread mixture.

9. Pour mixture into the prepared casserole dish.

10. Place in oven and bake uncovered for 30 to 40 minutes, or until the top is lightly browned.

MUSHROOM STUFFING

Intensely flavored mushrooms don't need much help when it comes to making this palate-pleasing holiday side dish.

SERVES 6-8 | PREP 20 MINS | COOK 1 HR 7 MINS

INGREDIENTS

2 tablespoons olive oil

8 ounces fresh cremini mushrooms, roughly chopped

1 cup wild mushrooms, fresh or reconstituted from dried, roughly chopped

1 medium onion, finely diced

2 stalks celery, finely diced

1-1/2 tablespoons fresh thyme leaves, minced

1 tablespoon finely chopped fresh Italian parsley

1 tablespoon minced sage

1/2 teaspoon freshly ground black pepper

1 loaf of gluten-free, vegan bread, cut into 2-inch pieces, dried or toasted

1 to 1-1/2 cups vegetable broth

1-1/2 teaspoons sea salt

INSTRUCTIONS

1. Preheat oven to 350F and spray a 9x13-inch baking dish with cooking spray.

2. In a large skillet over medium-high, heat olive oil. Add mushrooms, onions, celery, thyme, parsley, sage, salt and pepper. Cook, stirring often, for 6 to 7 minutes, or until the onions are soft and translucent. Remove from heat and set the mushroom mixture aside.

3. In a large bowl, mix dried bread cubes with 1 cup vegetable broth. If the mixture is too dry, continue adding broth in small increments until the bread is wet, but not soggy. Note: You may not use all the broth.

4. Add the mushroom mixture to the bread mixture and mix well.

5. Pour the stuffing mixture into the prepared baking dish.

6. Bake for 45 minutes to 1 hour or until the top of the stuffing is browned and crispy. Serve hot.

BRANDIED WILD RICE STUFFING WITH CORNBREAD AND PECANS

Abounding in mouthwatering flavors, this wild rice stuffing is satisfying, chewy and studded with bacon, mushrooms, dried apricots, pecans and fresh herbs.

SERVES 8-10 | PREP 20 MINS | COOK 50 MINS

INGREDIENTS

4 slices bacon, diced into 1/4-inch pieces

1 small onion, diced

3 cloves garlic, minced

1 cup diced celery

1 cup shiitake mushrooms, cleaned, sliced

1/3 cup minced Italian parsley

2 tablespoons chopped fresh sage

1-1/2 cups cooked wild rice

4 cups crumbled dry cornbread made without sugar

3/4 cup chopped pecans

3/4 cup butter, melted

1/2 cup diced dried apricots

1/2 cup chicken or vegetable broth, plus more as needed

1/4 teaspoon freshly ground black pepper

1/2 cup brandy

INSTRUCTIONS

1. Preheat oven to 350F.

2. In a large heavy skillet over medium-high heat, cook bacon, stirring often, until browned. (Note: You can also use a large electric skillet heated to 350F.) Transfer the cooked bacon to a plate lined with paper towels to drain.

3. To the skillet, with the bacon grease, add onions, garlic and celery. Cook, stirring occasionally, for 8 minutes, or until the onions are glossy.

4. Add the mushrooms, Italian parsley and sage. Cook, stirring occasionally, for another 8 minutes.

5. Add the wild rice, cornbread, pecans, butter, apricots, chicken or vegetable broth and black pepper to the vegetable mixture. Stir well to combine the stuffing ingredients.

6. Pour brandy over the stuffing and cook for 3 to 4 minutes. Add more broth to the stuffing, if it is too dry.

7. Stir in the cooked bacon pieces.

8. Transfer the stuffing to a buttered casserole dish.

9. Bake for 20 to 25 minutes.

10. Remove the stuffing from the oven and serve hot.

tip / Streamline your meal prep by cooking the wild rice and making the cornbread up to 3 days in advance.

MAPLE BACON ROASTED BRUSSELS SPROUTS

This recipe combines Brussels sprouts with bacon and maple syrup to complement all those seasonal dishes on your table.

SERVES 4 | PREP 15 MINS | COOK 23 MINS

INGREDIENTS

3 strips thick-cut bacon, chopped

2 tablespoons pure maple syrup

2 teaspoons apple cider vinegar

2 teaspoons grainy mustard

1 pound small Brussels sprouts, stem ends removed

INSTRUCTIONS

1. Place a cast-iron skillet in the oven and preheat both to 500F. Once the oven and skillet have preheated, carefully remove the skillet from the oven.

2. Add the chopped bacon pieces, spreading them evenly around the bottom of the skillet.

3. Place the skillet back in the oven and cook for 8 minutes or until the bacon is done. Make sure the bacon doesn't burn.

4. In a small bowl, whisk together the maple syrup, vinegar and mustard.

5. Remove the skillet of bacon from the oven and add the Brussels sprouts. Stir to coat them in bacon fat.

6. Return the skillet to the oven and cook for 15 minutes. Watch carefully so they don't get overly crispy.

7. Remove the skillet from the oven and pour the maple syrup mixture over the bacon and sprouts. Stir to evenly coat the ingredients.

8. Serve warm.

ROASTED CARROTS WITH INDIAN SPICES, CREAMY DRESSING AND WALNUT PARSLEY TOPPING

Drizzled with a creamy, lemony dressing and topped with chopped walnuts, parsley and Indian spices, these carrots are a showstopper.

SERVES 6-8 | PREP 25 MINS | COOK 45 MINS

INGREDIENTS

Carrots

1 teaspoon ground cumin

1 teaspoon ground ginger

1/2 teaspoon red pepper flakes

1/3 cup orange juice

3 tablespoons extra-virgin olive oil

1-1/2 tablespoons sherry vinegar

2 tablespoons honey

2 pounds assorted carrots in various colors, peeled and trimmed with partial tops and stems left intact

Salt and pepper, to taste

1/4 cup toasted walnuts, chopped

1/4 cup Italian parsley, roughly chopped

Creamy dressing

3/4 cup plain French or Greek yogurt

1 cup parsley

1 garlic clove, minced

1 tablespoon lemon juice

1/2 teaspoon ground coriander

Salt and pepper, to taste

INSTRUCTIONS

Carrots

1. Preheat oven to 425F.

2. In small skillet, toast ground cumin, ground ginger and red pepper flakes until fragrant. Remove from heat and set aside.

3. In small bowl, combine orange juice, oil, sherry vinegar and honey with carrots. Toss well with toasted spices, salt and pepper.

4. Lay carrots on 2 rimmed baking sheets lined with parchment paper, spread out, not touching. Bake about 15 minutes. Then, rotate pans in oven and continue baking until tender, approximately 25–30 minutes.

5. Once carrots can be pierced with a fork easily, remove from heat and set aside.

Creamy dressing

1. In small bowl, whisk yogurt, parsley, garlic, lemon juice, ground coriander, salt and pepper until well-mixed.

2. Place carrots on serving platter.

3. Drizzle creamy dressing on top of carrots.

4. Before serving, garnish with toasted walnuts and additional parsley, if desired.

Recipe by Katie Higgins

ROASTED BUTTERNUT SQUASH

This recipe is flexible. Swap in dried cranberries for the raisins or add crushed walnuts. It's perfect for customizing.

SERVES 6-8 | PREP 5 MINS | COOK 50 MINS

INGREDIENTS

5 cups peeled, cubed butternut squash or sweet potatoes

2 cups diced apples

1/2 cup raisins or dried cranberries

2 teaspoons cinnamon

1/2 teaspoon salt

Sweetener of choice, such as 2 tablespoons pure maple syrup or pinch stevia

1 tablespoon oil, for richness (optional)

INSTRUCTIONS

1. Stir all of the ingredients together (except the sweetener if using a liquid sweetener).

2. Spread mixture out in one large baking dish, or two medium baking dishes, lined with parchment paper.

3. Place on the center rack of an unheated oven, then turn to 480F. Bake 40 minutes.

4. Stir, return to the oven, and close the door.

5. Turn off the heat but leave in the closed oven an additional 10 minutes.

6. Remove from oven and stir in the sweetener, if using a liquid.

HONEY BUTTER ROASTED ACORN SQUASH

The honey, thyme and butter roasted with this squash deliver a mouthwatering medley of sweet and savory.

SERVES 2-3 | PREP 15 MINS | COOK 30 MINS

INGREDIENTS

2 tablespoons butter, melted

2 tablespoons honey

1/4 teaspoon cayenne pepper

2 whole acorn squash, seeded, unpeeled, sliced

1 teaspoon salt

1/2 teaspoon freshly ground black pepper

1 tablespoon fresh thyme leaves, minced

INSTRUCTIONS

1. Preheat oven to 400F.

2. In a small bowl, whisk together the melted butter, honey and cayenne pepper.

3. Place the sliced squash in a large bowl. Pour the honey butter mixture over the squash and toss until all the squash slices are coated.

4. Line 2 baking sheets with parchment paper.

5. Arrange the acorn squash onto the baking sheets, spreading the slices out so they aren't touching.

6. Season the squash with salt, black pepper and minced thyme leaves.

7. Bake for 30 minutes, or until the squash is soft when pierced with a fork.

8. Remove from oven.

9. Serve immediately.

Turkey

ROSEMARY TURKEY BREAST ROASTED IN AN OVEN BAG

If you're a fan of white meat, this turkey breast recipe is just what you need and nothing more.

SERVES 4-6 | PREP 20 MINS | COOK 3 HRS 20 MINS

INGREDIENTS

One (5 to 7 pound) turkey breast

2 lemons, cut into quarters

1 large onion, cut into eighths

1 kitchen oven roasting bag and tie

1 to 1-1/2 cups chicken stock

1/2 cup melted butter

1-1/2 tablespoons rosemary, minced

Salt and pepper

INSTRUCTIONS

1. Preheat oven to 350F.

2. Pat the turkey dry with paper towels to remove excess moisture.

3. Fold and roll back the bag around the top three times.

4. Place the cut up lemons and onions in a pile in the center of the roasting bag.

5. Pour the chicken stock into the bottom of the roasting bag.

6. Place turkey breast inside of bag on top of the onions and lemons.

7. Brush melted butter all over the turkey breast coating the skin inside and on top of the breast.

8. Sprinkle the rosemary over the top of the breast. Season with salt and pepper.

9. Close roasting bag with closure that accompanied the browning bag. Do not close the bag too tightly as the bag will expand during the cooking process.

10. Move the oven rack low enough in the oven to allow room for the bag to puff up without touching the top of the oven during the roasting process. Place turkey breast in the oven.

11. Bake at 350F. Total time should be 2 1/2 to 3 hours depending upon size of the turkey breast. The internal temperature in the thickest part of the breast should reach 165F.

12. Remove from oven. Allow the turkey breast to rest for at least 20 minutes.

13. Remove the turkey from bag and place on chopping board. Slice turkey and serve. The cooking liquid can be reserved to use for gravy.

CAJUN-SPICED DEEP FRIED TURKEY

While a roasted bird is always delicious, a deep-fried bird is a gourmet-level experience.

SERVES 8-10 | PREP 25 MINS | COOK 1 HR 10 MINS

INGREDIENTS

4 tablespoons onion powder

4 tablespoons garlic powder

4 tablespoons salt

2 tablespoons red pepper flakes

2 tablespoons smoky paprika

1 tablespoon ground oregano

1 cup of butter

3 gallons peanut oil

One (10 to 12 pound) turkey, thawed

INSTRUCTIONS

1. Pour peanut oil into deep fat fryer.
2. Heat peanut oil until temperature reaches 350F.
3. Mix spices together in a small bowl.
4. Melt butter in a small saucepan.
5. Add spices to the butter and mix well.
6. Fill the meat injector with the butter mixture.
7. Pull the skin back from the breast meat and inject the butter spice mixture into several areas of the turkey.
8. Repeat this process two to three times.
9. Rub the remaining spice butter mixture inside and outside of the turkey.
10. Carefully lower the turkey into the hot oil, making certain that it is fully submerged.
11. Fry turkey for three minutes per pound, plus an extra five minutes.
12. Remove turkey from hot oil. Drain on paper towels. Allow to rest for 10 to 15 minutes.
13. Carve and serve.

BACON-WRAPPED TURKEY

Take a traditional turkey and make it the star of the show by wrapping it with crispy, smoky bacon.

SERVES 8-10 | PREP 35 MINS | COOK 3 HRS 20 MINS TO 4 HRS 50 MINS (INCLUDING RESTING TIME)

INGREDIENTS

10 slices applewood smoked bacon, divided

1 medium onion, finely chopped

2 tablespoons finely chopped fresh sage

1 (12-pound) turkey, thawed if frozen

Kosher salt and freshly ground black pepper

1/2 cup butter, melted

2 to 3 sprigs fresh sage

1 medium sweet onion, cut into wedges

1 bulb garlic, cloves separated, skin removed

2 oranges, sliced

1 small bunch fresh parsley, with stems

1 cup chicken broth

INSTRUCTIONS

1. Preheat oven to 325F.

2. Finely chop two slices of bacon.

3. In a small bowl, combine the chopped bacon, chopped onion and chopped fresh sage. Set aside.

4. Remove the giblets and neck bone from inside of the turkey and, optionally, place them in the bottom of the roasting pan. Otherwise, discard.

5. After rinsing the turkey well, pat it dry with paper towels.

6. Loosen the breast skin of the turkey by sliding your fingers underneath it, ensuring that you don't tear the skin. Separate the skin from the meat as far back under the breast as possible. Rub the bacon mixture underneath the skin and over the entire breast, reaching down toward the thigh bones.

7. Salt and pepper the inside of the cavity of the turkey. Fill the cavity with extra sage, sweet onion wedges, garlic cloves, orange slices and fresh parsley.

8. Pull the neck skin back and over the cavity and secure with a bamboo skewer.

9. Tuck the wings under the turkey. Tie the legs together with cotton twine.

10. Place turkey breast side up on a rack in a roasting pan.

11. Brush melted butter over the entire breast, sides and legs of the turkey. Salt and pepper the outside.

12. Weave eight strips of bacon in a lattice pattern over the breast. Tuck additional sage leaves underneath the bacon weave.

13. Add extra onions, oranges and garlic to the bottom of the pan.

14. Pour the chicken broth into the bottom of the pan.

15. Cover pan loosely with foil and place it in the oven.

16. Roast for 2-1/2 hours. Remove foil. Roast for another 30 minutes to 1-1/2 hours. The turkey is done when a thermometer inserted into the thigh reaches 180F.

17. Remove the turkey from the oven and cover with foil. Allow to rest for 20 minutes.

18. Carve and serve.

ROSEMARY LEMON ROASTED TURKEY

Succulent and juicy, this roasted turkey recipe boasts buttery goodness with rosemary, lemon, garlic and onion flavors.

SERVES 10-12 | PREP 25 MINS | COOK 3 HRS 20 MINS TO 4 HOURS 50 MINS (INCLUDING RESTING TIME)

INGREDIENTS

1 cup olive oil

4 garlic cloves, chopped

Zest and juice of one large lemon

2 tablespoons minced fresh rosemary

One (15-pound) turkey, neck and giblets removed

1/2 cup butter, cut into slices, softened

Salt and freshly ground black pepper

2 cups of your favorite stuffing, cooked

1 large onion, cut into two-inch pieces

2 cups chicken broth, plus extra as needed

INSTRUCTIONS

1. Preheat oven to 400F. Set the oven rack on a low position in the oven.

2. In a small saucepan over medium-low heat, combine olive oil, garlic, lemon zest and rosemary. Cook until hot. Remove from heat and set aside while you prepare the turkey.

3. Place the turkey in a roasting pan.

4. Prepare the turkey by adding salt and pepper inside the large cavity.

5. Add about 1-1/2 cups of stuffing inside the large cavity.

6. Add the rest of the stuffing inside the smaller cavity on other end of the turkey.

7. Using your fingers, separate the skin from the breast meat, starting at the top of the breast and sliding to the right and left, then working down.

8. Arrange the pieces of butter under the skin and onto the meat.

9. Tie the turkey legs together and tuck the wing tips under.

10. Squeeze lemon juice all over the turkey.

11. Brush the turkey with half of the infused herb and olive oil.

12. Season the entire turkey with salt and pepper.

13. Place onions in the bottom of the roasting pan, along with 1-1/2 cups of chicken broth. Optional: Add giblets if desired.

14. Roast the turkey for one hour.

15. Reduce heat to 375F.

16. Tent foil over the turkey and continue to roast for 2 to 3-1/2 hours or until a thermometer inserted into the breast reads 165F.

17. While the turkey is roasting, brush turkey with remaining infused olive oil every 30 minutes.

18. Add more chicken broth, one cup at a time, if the roasting pan becomes dry.

19. Transfer the turkey to a serving platter and let it rest for 20 minutes.

20. Carve and serve.

MAYONNAISE ROASTED TURKEY

An herb-laden blanket of mayo transforms this turkey into the most irresistibly glistening and succulent dish on the menu.

SERVES 10-12 | PREP 25 MINS | COOK 3 HRS 20 MINS TO 4 HRS 50 MINS

INGREDIENTS

One (12 to 14 pound) whole turkey, thawed, neck and giblets removed

1-1/2 cups of mayonnaise

2 tablespoons minced fresh sage leaves, plus extra whole leaves

2 tablespoons minced fresh thyme leaves, plus extra whole stems of leaves

2 tablespoons minced rosemary, plus extra whole sprigs

2 tablespoons minced fresh oregano, plus extra whole sprigs

2 tablespoons coarse salt

1 tablespoon freshly ground black pepper

3 stalks celery, roughly chopped

1 large onion, roughly chopped

1/2 cup butter, cubed

2 cups chicken broth, plus more if needed

INSTRUCTIONS

1. Preheat the oven to 450F.

2. Place turkey on a roasting rack in a roasting pan.

3. Tie the turkey legs together with twine and tuck the wings underneath.

4. In a small bowl, stir together mayonnaise, minced sage, thyme, rosemary and oregano.

5. Rub mayonnaise and herb mixture all over the outside of the turkey.

6. Season the turkey with salt and pepper.

7. Place celery and onion inside the turkey cavity and drop extra pieces in the bottom of the roasting pan.

8. Place the cubed butter inside turkey cavity. Add the additional whole herbs.

9. Pour two cups chicken broth into bottom of roasting pan. Continue to add broth or water as turkey is roasting if the pan becomes dry.

10. Roast turkey for one hour at 450F. Reduce oven heat to 350F and continue roasting, uncovered, until internal thermometer reaches 165F for breasts. Cover legs and breasts with foil halfway through cooking process if the turkey begins getting too brown.

11. Remove turkey from the oven. Cover loosely with foil and allow to rest for at least 20 minutes before carving.

12. Carve and serve.

ORANGE BOURBON SLOW-COOKER TURKEY BREAST

Every juicy bite of this slow-cooked turkey delivers a delicious combination of warm spices, brown sugar, orange juice, bourbon and honey.

SERVES 4-6 | PREP 20 MINS | COOK 4 HRS 20 MINS TO 5 HRS 20 MINS (INCLUDING RESTING TIME)

INGREDIENTS

1-1/2 teaspoons sweet paprika

1-1/2 teaspoons salt

1 teaspoon garlic powder

1 teaspoon onion powder

1 teaspoon black pepper

1 teaspoon brown sugar

1/4 teaspoon cayenne pepper

1 teaspoon ground cumin, toasted

1/4 teaspoon ground cloves

1/2 cup bourbon

1/2 cup orange juice

2 tablespoons orange zest

1/2 cup honey

3 to 4 pound turkey breast, skin removed

1 orange, cut into quarters

INSTRUCTIONS

1. In a small bowl, whisk together the paprika, salt, garlic powder, onion powder, black pepper, brown sugar, cayenne pepper, toasted cumin and ground cloves. Set aside.

2. In a separate small bowl, whisk together the bourbon, orange juice, orange zest and honey. Set aside.

3. Rub the spice mixture over the entire outside of the turkey breast.

4. Add orange wedges to the bottom of the slow-cooker. Place turkey breast in the slow-cooker.

5. Pour the bourbon mixture over the turkey.

6. Turn the slow-cooker to high and cook turkey breast for four to five hours. Turkey is done when a thermometer inserted in the center of the breast reaches 165F.

7. Transfer the turkey breast to a cutting board and allow it to rest for 20 minutes.

8. Carve the turkey breast into slices. Serve hot.

CLASSIC ROASTED TURKEY

This traditionally roasted bird is butter-basted and stuffed with a generous number of lemon wedges and bunches of fresh herbs.

SERVES 8-10 | PREP 40 MINS | 3 HRS 15 MINS +

INGREDIENTS

One (12 to 14 pound) turkey

3 lemons, divided

1 bunch fresh parsley

1 bunch fresh tarragon leaves

4 tablespoons
softened butter

9 to 10 strips fresh salt pork

1 teaspoons salt

1 teaspoon freshly
ground pepper

1 stick butter, divided, melted

INSTRUCTIONS

1. Preheat oven to 350F.

2. Rub the inside of the turkey with lemon halves. Stuff the inside of the turkey with lemon quarters and a small bunch each of parsley and tarragon.

3. Tie the legs of the turkey together.

4. Using 4 tablespoons butter, massage the turkey all over. Line a roasting rack with strips of fresh salt pork.

5. Set the rack in a fairly shallow roasting pan and place the turkey breast-side down on the rack. Season the turkey with salt and pepper. Roast for one hour.

6. Remove the turkey from the oven. Rotate the turkey to one side and brush with 2 tablespoons melted butter. Roast for another hour.

7. Remove the turkey from the oven, turn the turkey to the other side and brush with 2 tablespoons melted butter. Roast for another hour.

8. Turn the turkey onto its back and brush the breast with the remaining 2 tablespoons melted butter. Return the turkey to the oven and continue roasting until the internal temperature of the turkey reaches 165F.

9. Remove the turkey from the oven and place it on a serving platter. Allow it to rest for 15 minutes before carving.

EASY NO-FUSS HOLIDAY TURKEY

Whether you're new to cooking turkey or simply want a fast, fail-proof way to prepare the proverbial bird, this fuss-free turkey is a crowd-pleaser.

SERVES 10 | PREP 30 MINS | COOK TIME BASED ON TURKEY SIZE

INGREDIENTS

For herb butter

1 cup unsalted butter, softened

1 teaspoon salt

1 teaspoon freshly ground black pepper

8 cloves garlic, minced

1 tablespoon minced fresh rosemary

1 tablespoon minced fresh thyme leaves

1 tablespoon minced fresh sage leaves

For turkey

One (12 to 16 pound) thawed turkey, at room temperature for 1 hour

1 teaspoon salt

1/2 teaspoon freshly ground black pepper

1/4 cup fresh rosemary sprigs

1/4 cup fresh thyme sprigs

1/4 cup fresh sage leaves

1 yellow onion, peeled, cut in eighths

1 lemon, cut in eighths

1 red apple, cored, cut into eighths

INSTRUCTIONS

1. Preheat oven to 325F.

2. In a small bowl, combine butter, salt, pepper, minced garlic and one tablespoon each of minced rosemary, thyme and sage. Blend with a spatula and set aside.

3. Pat the turkey dry with paper towels inside and outside the cavity.

4. Season the cavity of the turkey with one teaspoon salt and 1/2 teaspoon pepper.

5. Use your fingers to loosen and lift the skin attached to the breast. Insert half of the herb butter underneath the skin against the turkey flesh.

6. Tuck the wings of the turkey underneath the turkey and set the turkey on a rack inside a roasting pan.

7. Stuff the cavity of the turkey with the quartered onion, lemon and apple. Insert the 1/4 cup each of fresh rosemary, thyme and sage.

8. Use twine to tie the turkey legs together.

9. Melt the remaining herb butter mixture in the microwave for 30 seconds.

10. Use a basting brush to coat the remaining herb butter all over the outside of the turkey, legs and wings.

11. Roast the turkey until the internal temperature reaches 165F.

12. Rotate the roasting pan several times while the turkey roasts to ensure even cooking and browning. Once the skin turns golden brown, cover the top of the turkey with foil to protect the breast meat from overcooking.

13. Allow the turkey to rest for 15 minutes before carving.

14. Carve and serve.

ORANGE ANISE & THYME ROASTED TURKEY

This roasted turkey is not only covered under the skin with a garlicky citrus compound butter, it's stuffed with a combination of aromatics for a flavor infusion.

SERVES 10 | PREP 1 HR 30 MINS (INCLUDES 1 HR RESTING/DRYING OF TURKEY) COOK TIME VARIES

INGREDIENTS

One (14 to 15 pound) turkey

4 large oranges, zest and juice in separate bowls, divided

5 cloves garlic, minced

3 tablespoons fresh thyme leaves

1-1/2 tablespoons salt

2 tablespoons dark brown sugar

1/2 teaspoon freshly ground black pepper

1 cup butter, softened

1 orange, cut into slices

1 red onion, cut into 6 chunks

5 whole star anise pods

2 to 3 fresh thyme sprigs

INSTRUCTIONS

1. Preheat oven to 350F.

2. Prepare the turkey by drying it with paper towels. Allow the turkey to sit at room temperature for one hour.

3. In the bowl of a small food processor, combine orange zest, garlic, thyme leaves, salt, dark brown sugar and black pepper. Pulse until the mixture forms a coarse paste.

4. Scrape the paste into a bowl with softened butter and use a spatula to mix it until well combined.

5. Loosen the skin of the turkey with your fingers. Smear the herb butter under the skin and all over the turkey breast. Add more butter to the legs, sides and outside breast of the turkey.

6. Stuff the cavity of the turkey with orange slices, red onion pieces, star anise, thyme sprigs and any leftover herb butter.

7. Fill the turkey injector with the orange juice.

8. Inject the orange juice into all areas of the turkey.

9. Place the turkey in the oven and cook until the internal temperature of the breast reaches 165F.

10. Remove the turkey from the oven and allow it to rest for 15 minutes.

11. Place the turkey on a serving platter. Garnish with additional orange slices and fresh thyme leaves.

12. Carve and serve.

TOFURKEY WITH MUSHROOM STUFFING AND GRAVY

The vegans in your life don't have to miss out at your next holiday feast. This tofurkey is a showstopper—robust with texture and flavor..

SERVES 8 | PREP 1 HR 15 MINS | COOK 1 HR 46 MINS

INGREDIENTS

Tofurkey and glaze

6 tablespoons vegetable oil, divided

1/2 French demi baguette (about 4-1/2 ounces), cut into 1/4-inch cubes (about 3 cups)

1/2 cup raw pecans, coarsely chopped

1/2 medium onion, diced

1 garlic clove, finely diced

5 sprigs fresh thyme

8 ounces crimini mushrooms, coarsely chopped

1 large celery stalk, sliced crosswise into 1/4-inch thick pieces (about 1/2 cup)

1 cup homemade vegetable stock

1/3 cup dry white wine

3-1/2 teaspoons kosher salt, divided

1 teaspoon freshly ground black pepper, divided

3-1/2 tablespoons soy sauce, divided

1 tablespoon pure maple syrup

1/2 teaspoon smoked paprika

1/8 teaspoon cayenne pepper

3 (14-ounce) packages extra-firm

tofu, drained, squeezed in a clean towel until moisture is minimal

3 tablespoons white miso paste

2 tablespoons cornstarch

1 teaspoon garlic powder

1 tablespoon chopped fresh parsley

Gravy

3 tablespoons vegetable oil, divided

12 ounces crimini mushrooms, coarsely chopped

2 shallots, minced

1 garlic clove, roughly chopped

5 sprigs thyme

2 fresh bay leaves

3 cups vegetable broth

2 tablespoons all-purpose flour

1/2 cup dry white wine

1 tablespoon coarsely chopped parsley

1 1/2 teaspoons kosher salt, plus more

1/4 teaspoon freshly ground black pepper, plus more

INSTRUCTIONS

Tofurkey and glaze

1. Preheat oven to 425F.

2. Place 2 tablespoons of vegetable oil, bread and pecans in a large bowl and toss to combine.

3. Spread the bread and pecans in a single layer on a rimmed baking sheet lined with parchment paper. Bake for 8 to 10 minutes or until the bread is light golden brown and dry.

4. In a large skillet over medium heat, heat 2 tablespoons of vegetable oil.

5. Add onion, garlic and thyme to the skillet. Cook, stirring often, for 5 minutes or until the onion is translucent.

6. Add the mushrooms and cook, stirring often, for 5 minutes or until they are just beginning to brown.

7. Add celery and cook, stirring often, until the mushrooms are cooked through, about 3 minutes more.

8. Remove the thyme sprigs and transfer the mushroom mixture to a large bowl.

9. Increase the heat to medium-high. Pour stock and wine into the hot skillet to deglaze the pan, scraping up the browned bits. Season with 1 teaspoon salt and 1/2 teaspoon black pepper. Cook, stirring, until just combined, about 1 minute.

10. Add the bread and pecans to the mushroom mixture, tossing to combine.

11. Pour the stock mixture over the bread mixture and toss well to combine.

12. In a small bowl, whisk remaining 2 tablespoons vegetable oil, 2 tablespoons soy sauce, maple syrup, paprika, cayenne and 1/2 teaspoon salt in a medium bowl. Set aside.

13. Place tofu in a food processor. Add the remaining 1-1/2 tablespoons of soy sauce, miso, cornstarch, garlic powder and remaining 2 teaspoons of salt and 1/2 teaspoon of black pepper. Blend on high for 30 seconds or until the mixture is smooth.

14. Brush a 9x5-inch loaf pan with additional vegetable oil. Line it with a sheet of parchment paper, cut to fit the pan horizontally. Brush the entire pan and parchment with oil.

15. Using an oiled spatula, line the bottom and interior sides of the prepared pan with two-thirds of the tofu mixture, pressing it firmly to create compact high walls in the pan.

16. Spoon the mushroom mixture into the center and press down firmly. Cover with remaining tofu mixture and smooth the surface.

17. Brush one-third of the glaze over top of the tofurkey.

18. Transfer the loaf pan to a rimmed baking sheet and bake the tofurkey for 30 minutes, brushing the top with glaze after it has baked for 15 minutes. The tofurkey should be lightly browned.

19. Line another rimmed baking sheet with parchment paper and place it over the loaf pan. Quickly and carefully invert the pans to transfer the tofurkey onto the baking sheet.

20. Gently remove the parchment paper and brush the tofurkey all over with the remaining glaze.

21. To darken the top of the tofurkey, broil it for 6 to 7 minutes or until a light brown crust forms. Cool at least 10 minutes. Garnish with fresh parsley and serve the tofurkey with the gravy on the side.

Vegan gravy

1. Heat 1 tablespoon of vegetable oil in a large saucepan over medium-low until it begins to brown and smells fragrant, about 30 seconds.

2. Add the mushrooms, shallot, garlic, thyme and bay leaves. Cook, stirring occasionally, for 5 minutes or until the mushrooms are tender and beginning to brown.

3. Pour in the stock and bring to a simmer. Cook, stirring occasionally, for 30 minutes or until the liquid is reduced by half.

4. Pour mushroom mixture into a strainer, reserving both liquid broth and mushrooms separately.

5. Add 2 tablespoons oil and 2 tablespoons flour to skillet and toast over medium heat, stirring constantly, until browned and thickened, 5–7 minutes.

6. Add wine, stir to combine, and cook 30 seconds. Whisk in mushroom broth, 1 1/2 teaspoon salt, and 1/4 teaspoon pepper and bring to a simmer over medium-low heat. Cook, stirring occasionally, until slightly reduced and thickened, about 10 minutes.

7. Place entire contents of broth and reserved mushrooms into a blender. Turn on high speed until well blended. Pour back into pot and keep warm.

8. Garnish with minced parsley and serve with mushroom gravy.

Find more vegan recipes at
thanksgiving.com/tag/vegan

Mains

GARLIC HERB-CRUSTED ROAST BEEF

This roast takes just minutes of hands-on time to prepare.

SERVES 4-6 | PREP 15 MINS | COOK 1 HR TO 1 HR 15 MINS

INGREDIENTS

2-1/2 pounds beef eye of round roast

1 tablespoon black peppercorns, crushed

2 tablespoons chopped fresh basil

4-1/2 teaspoons chopped fresh thyme

2 tablespoons chopped fresh rosemary

2 tablespoons minced fresh garlic

1-1/2 teaspoons coarse salt

INSTRUCTIONS

1. Preheat oven to 425F.

2. Place the roast in the meat rack of a shallow roasting pan.

3. In a small bowl, mix cracked peppercorns, basil, thyme, rosemary and garlic.

4. Rub the spice mixture completely over the sides and around the top of the roast.

5. Roast for 50 to 60 minutes, or until the internal temperature of the roast is 135F for medium rare or 150F for medium.

6. Transfer the roast to a cutting board. Cover the roast with foil and allow it to rest for 10 to 15 minutes. The internal temperature of the roast will rise another 5 to 10 degrees.

7. To serve, cut the roast into 1/2-inch slices.

tip Beef eye of round roast is an inexpensive, lean and flavorful cut requiring longer, slower roasting times to achieve tenderness. You could also use bottom round roast and sirloin tip roast.

SLOW-COOKED PRIME RIB WITH HORSERADISH CREAM SAUCE

This tender slow-cooked prime rib with a creamy horseradish sauce is so mouthwatering, no one will miss the bird.

SERVES 8-10 | PREP 1 HR 15 MINS + OVERNIGHT | COOK 3 HRS 36 MINS TO 5 HRS 40 MINS

INGREDIENTS

Prime rib

8- to 10-pound standing rib roast (prime rib), bones frenched

Kosher salt

Freshly ground black pepper

1-1/2 tablespoons fresh thyme

Horseradish sauce

1/2 cup heavy cream

1/2 cup sour cream

1/2 cup prepared horseradish

2 tablespoons chives, minced

1 tablespoon freshly squeezed lemon juice

Salt, to taste

Freshly ground black pepper, to taste

INSTRUCTIONS

1. Place a v-rack in a roasting pan. Place rib roast on top of v-rack and generously sprinkle salt all over and under roast.

2. Allow to stand in refrigerator, uncovered, overnight or up to two days.

3. Preheat oven to 250F.

4. When ready to roast, sprinkle meat with freshly ground pepper and thyme on all sides.

5. Cook in oven three to four hours until the center of roast registers 125F on an instant-read thermometer for medium-rare or 135F degrees for medium.

6. When roast is cooked, remove from oven and tent loosely with aluminum foil.

7. Allow the meat to rest for 30 to 90 minutes.

8. Ten minutes before serving, increase oven temperature to the highest setting (500F-550F).

9. Remove foil from prime rib.

10. Return roast to hot oven and cook for another 6-10 minutes. Watch carefully to ensure it does not burn.

11. Remove from oven, carve off bones and slice roast.

12. Serve immediately with horseradish sauce.

Horseradish sauce (yields 1-1/2 cups)

1. In a medium bowl, whisk heavy cream with a handheld mixer until thickened but not yet at soft-peak level.

2. Fold in sour cream, horseradish, chives, lemon juice, salt and pepper, and mix well.

3. Refrigerate for 30 to 60 minutes before serving, or transfer to airtight container and refrigerate up to two weeks.

PAN-SEARED FILET MIGNON WITH SHALLOT BUTTER

If you're making a meal for two, go gourmet with filet mignon. It's lean yet packed with flavor and melt-in-your-mouth texture when cooked properly to rare or medium-rare.

SERVES 2 | PREP 10 MINS PLUS 40 MINS TO 2 HRS OF RESTING TIME | COOK TIME VARIES

INGREDIENTS

2 filet mignons, at least
1-1/2 inches thick

Kosher salt

Freshly ground black pepper

2 tablespoons avocado oil

2 tablespoons butter

1 whole shallot, sliced thin

1 tablespoon fresh thyme

INSTRUCTIONS

1. Using paper towels, pat steaks dry on both sides. Season liberally with salt. Allow to rest at room temperature for at least 40 minutes and up to 2 hours before cooking.

2. Heat oil in cast-iron skillet over high heat until smoking.

3. Season steaks with pepper and add to skillet. Cook for 4 to 5 minutes. Flip and continue to cook until internal temperature has reached 110F for rare or 130F for medium.

4. Remove steaks from skillet and tent loosely with foil. Set aside. Allow to rest at least 5 minutes before serving.

5. Add butter and shallots to skillet, lower temperature to medium, and continue cooking for an additional few minutes until shallots are translucent. Add thyme and allow to cook for 30 seconds.

6. Spoon melted butter mixture from pan over steaks and serve.

tip / To get the perfect sear on a steak, you must use a fat with a high smoke point, like the avocado oil in this recipe, to give your filet mignon a deliciously seasoned crust and a tender, juicy center.

PORK TENDERLOIN WITH SWEET AND SPICY RUB

Every bite of this tender, juicy pork is full of sweet, spicy flavor that's hard to beat and totally worthy of a special occasion.

SERVES 8 | PREP 10 MINS PLUS 1 HR TO OVERNIGHT TO MARINATE PORK
COOK 30 MINS, OR UNTIL PROPER TEMP IS REACHED, PLUS 15 MINS TO REST

INGREDIENTS

1 cup dark brown sugar, packed

1/4 cup smoky paprika

1/4 cup fine sea salt

2 tablespoons fresh cracked peppercorns

1 tablespoon cayenne pepper

1 tablespoon dry mustard

2 tablespoons garlic powder

2 whole pork tenderloins

INSTRUCTIONS

1. Preheat oven to 325F.

2. With a whisk, mix sugar and spices in large bowl.

3. Pour 1/2 cup of this rub mix into a large zip top bag; place pork tenderloins into the bag. Add another 1/2 cup rub mix on top of pork, then shake to combine, making sure to cover the pork completely.

4. To allow the spice flavors to penetrate the meat, place the plastic bag in the refrigerator and allow it to sit for at least 1 hour or overnight.

5. When you're ready to cook, use nonstick cooking spray to coat the inverted rack of your roasting pan.

6. Place the tenderloins onto the roasting rack.

7. Roast the pork at 325F for about 25 to 30 minutes, or until the meat's internal temperature reaches 140F. If you don't have a meat thermometer, cook only until the loin feels firm and springs back when pressed with your finger and the juices run clear when poked with a knife.

8. Remove from oven and allow to rest for 15 minutes before slicing.

tip / The longer you can allow the tenderloins to sit in the refrigerator, the more the flavors of the rub can penetrate and fully develop.

ROAST PORK LOIN WITH DRIED FRUITS

Pork loin becomes a seasonal feast with the addition of cherries, figs and apricots.

SERVES 6-8 | PREP 45 MINS | COOK 60-70 MINS PLUS 15 MINS RESTING TIME

INGREDIENTS

1 cup dried cherries

1 cup dried figs, cut in half

1 cup dried apricots, cut in half

2-1/2 cups merlot or cabernet sauvignon red wine

3 sticks cinnamon

2-1/2 tablespoons fresh rosemary, finely chopped

1-1/2 tablespoons parsley, finely chopped

1-1/2 teaspoon salt

1 teaspoon black pepper

3 cloves garlic, minced

2 tablespoons extra-virgin olive oil

3-1/2 to 4-pound boneless pork loin roast

INSTRUCTIONS

1. Preheat oven to 400F.

2. In small saucepan, place dried fruit, wine and cinnamon sticks, and bring to a boil.

3. Remove from heat and allow to steep 20–30 minutes.

4. Strain fruit, reserving liquid. Discard cinnamon sticks.

5. In small bowl, mix rosemary, parsley, salt, pepper and garlic.

6. Rub 2 tablespoons of mixture on inside of roast.

7. Layer with dried fruit and roll roast tightly into a log. Tie with butcher's twine to keep pork loin securely together.

8. Rub outside of roast with extra-virgin olive oil and remaining herb mixture.

9. Pour 1/2 cup of reserved wine liquid in bottom of roasting pan.

10. Place roast on V-rack in roasting pan.

11. Roast pork loin for 20 minutes, then reduce oven temperature to 325F.

12. Continue to roast until internal temperature reaches 155F, about 40 to 50 minutes.

13. Remove from oven and loosely drape with aluminum foil.

14. For juiciest tenderloin, let meat rest for 10 to 15 minutes before carving.

HONEY GLAZED BAKED HAM

Ham goes perfectly well with traditional sides like stuffing, mashed potatoes, and green beans.

SERVES 8-10 | PREP 20 MINS | COOK 1 HR 53 MINS

INGREDIENTS

2 tablespoons butter, melted

3 tablespoons honey

7- to 8-pound shank-cut half ham

1-1/2 cups granulated sugar

1/2 teaspoon seasoned salt

1/2 teaspoon onion powder

1/2 teaspoon ground cinnamon

1/2 teaspoon ground nutmeg

1/4 teaspoon ground ginger

1/4 teaspoon ground cloves

1/4 teaspoon paprika

Pinch of allspice

3 tablespoons juice from roasted ham

INSTRUCTIONS

1. Preheat oven to 275F.

2. In a small bowl, combine the melted butter and honey. Set aside.

3. Adjust the oven rack to the lower third position.

4. Line a roasting pan with a large and long strip of foil extending beyond the pan.

5. Position ham flat-side down in the center of the pan on a roasting rack.

6. Brush the entire ham with the honey butter mixture.

7. Bring the sides of the foil up over the ham and cover loosely. If needed, add a sheet of foil over the top to cover completely.

8. Bake the ham for approximately 12 to 15 minutes per pound. An 8-pound ham will take about 1 hour 30 minutes to 1 hour 40 minutes.

9. When done, remove the roasting pan from the oven. Remove 3 tablespoons ham juice from the bottom of the roasting pan.

10. In a small saucepan, combine the sugar, seasoned salt, onion powder, ground cinnamon, ground nutmeg, ground ginger, ground cloves, paprika and allspice. Heat on low until well-combined. Add the ham juice from the roasted ham and stir well. Boil juice for 1 minute, then remove from heat.

11. Remove the foil and brush glaze over the top and sides of the ham.

12. Place ham under the broiler for 1 to 3 minutes. It can burn quickly so watch closely.

13. Remove the ham from the oven and let rest for 5 to 10 minutes.

14. Slice the ham to serve. Drizzle the extra sauce over the slices. Serve warm or cold.

ORANGE PEPPER GLAZED BAKED HAM

This orange pepper glazed baked ham won't disappoint with its mouthwatering fusion of garlic, cloves, mustard, brown sugar, orange zest and wine.

SERVES 8 | PREP 20 MINS | COOK 1 HR 30 MIN

INGREDIENTS

10 to 12-pound ham

8 cloves of garlic, left whole

20 whole cloves

1 cup Riesling (sweet white wine)

1 cup orange juice

2 tablespoons orange zest

1/2 cup Dijon mustard

1/2 cup brown sugar

3 tablespoons marjoram, dried

1 tablespoon garlic powder

1-1/2 teaspoons black pepper, coarsely ground

1 cup chicken broth

INSTRUCTIONS

1. Preheat oven to 400F.
2. Trim excess fat off ham and score the top diagonally.
3. Place the ham in a large roasting pan over a V-rack.
4. Poke whole cloves throughout the diagonal scores of the ham.
5. Add garlic cloves to the bottom of the pan.
6. In a medium bowl, mix wine, orange juice and zest.
7. Pour orange juice mixture over ham.
8. Bake for 45 minutes.
9. In a medium bowl, blend together the Dijon mustard, brown sugar, marjoram, garlic powder, ground pepper and chicken broth.
10. Increase oven temperature to 450F.
11. Smear the entire ham with the mustard blend. Bake another 45 minutes, until the top is golden brown.
12. Pour off the excess juices and cook in the pan until thickened.
13. Serve extra drippings as a sauce for the ham.

CREAMY SALMON PICCATA

Our creamy salmon piccata will bring an unexpected twist to your holiday table.

SERVES 4 | PREP 25 MINS | COOK 12 MINS

INGREDIENTS

1 tablespoon olive oil

4 (6-ounce) skinless salmon fillets

Salt and freshly ground
black pepper

1 tablespoon garlic, minced

1-1/4 cups plus 1 tablespoon
chicken broth, divided

2 teaspoon cornstarch

1/3 cup heavy cream

2 tablespoons fresh lemon juice

1 tablespoon butter

1 tablespoon minced fresh dill

2 tablespoons capers, rinsed

1 tablespoon minced
fresh parsley

INSTRUCTIONS

1. Allow salmon to rest at room temperature 10 minutes.

2. Heat 12-inch heavy-bottomed nonstick skillet over medium-high heat. Add olive oil.

3. Dab salmon dry with paper towels. Season both sides lightly with salt and pepper.

4. Place in skillet and sear until bottom is golden brown, about 4 minutes. Carefully flip, then continue to cook until salmon is cooked through, about 2–3 minutes longer.

5. Transfer salmon to plate and cover with foil to keep warm, leaving about 1 teaspoon oil in skillet.

6. Add garlic and sauté just until golden brown, about 20 seconds.

7. Pour in 1-1/4 cups chicken broth and let simmer until broth is reduced by half, about 4 minutes. In a small bowl, whisk together remaining tablespoon of broth and the cornstarch.

8. While whisking, pour cornstarch mixture into reduced broth mixture. Cook and stir until thickened, about 1 minute.

9. Stir in cream, lemon juice, butter and dill. Remove from heat and return salmon to skillet.

10. Spoon sauce over salmon. Sprinkle with capers and parsley. Serve immediately.

tip / Capers finish this dish with a distinctive briny goodness. So don't be shy—they really make the dish.

GRILLED SALMON WITH MAPLE AND ROSEMARY

This non-traditional holiday main dish is still seasonal with flavors of maple and rosemary.

SERVES 6 | PREP 20 MINS | COOK 8-10 MINS

INGREDIENTS

1 large salmon fillet

1/4 cup extra-virgin olive oil

2 tablespoons maple syrup

1 teaspoon kosher salt

1/2 teaspoon freshly ground black pepper

2 teaspoons finely minced rosemary leaves, plus more for garnish

3 whole lemons, one thinly sliced, two cut in half

INSTRUCTIONS

1. Preheat the grill to medium.
2. Line a baking sheet with a large sheet of aluminum foil.
3. Lay the salmon fillet, skin side down, on the foil.
4. Generously brush olive oil all over the salmon flesh.
5. Brush the salmon with maple syrup.
6. Season the fish with salt and pepper.
7. Sprinkle the minced rosemary on top of fish.
8. Arrange the lemon slices on top of the salmon.
9. Fold the foil up on the sides to create walls that will keep the juices from spilling out.
10. Keeping the foil under and around the salmon, place onto the hot grill.
11. Close the grill lid and grill salmon for 8 to 10 minutes, or until internal temperature is 145F. Carefully remove the salmon from the grill and set aside.
12. Place the lemon halves directly on the hot grill and grill for 3 to 4 minutes or until the flesh is lightly charred.
13. Squeeze the grilled lemons over the top of the salmon and garnish with a sprinkling of minced fresh rosemary.
14. Serve hot.

VEGETABLE WELLINGTON

Adorn your table with this wow-worthy vegetarian main dish option, loaded with fresh vegetables and baked in a loaf pan for a spectacularly festive presentation.

SERVES 8-10 | PREP 55 MINS | COOK 1 HR 59 MINS

INGREDIENTS

3 tablespoons olive oil, divided, plus extra for coating pan

5 medium carrots, peeled, cut into 4-inch sticks

1 teaspoon salt, extra to taste

Pepper to taste

2 tablespoons fresh thyme leaves

1 pound asparagus, trimmed of hard stalks, cut into 1-1/2-inch pieces

1-1/2 large red bell peppers, seeded, cut into thin strips

1 medium onion, thinly sliced

1 (5-ounce) package fresh baby spinach leaves

4 ounces basil pesto sauce

1 large egg

1 (17.3-ounce) package frozen puff pastry, thawed

4 ounces fresh goat cheese, crumbled

1 (16-ounce) jar prepared tomato sauce

INSTRUCTIONS

1. Preheat oven to 400F.

2. Place carrots in a large skillet and cover with cold water. Season with salt. Bring to a boil over high heat and cook until the carrots are tender and most of the water has evaporated. Drain the water and transfer the cooked carrots to a baking dish.

3. Season the cooked carrots with salt and pepper. Sprinkle with thyme and drizzle with 2 tablespoons of olive oil then toss to coat. Roast the carrots, turning occasionally, for 30 minutes or until the carrots are lightly caramelized and wrinkled in appearance.

4. Remove the carrots from the oven and set aside.

5. Heat the remaining 2 tablespoons of oil in a large skillet over medium-high heat. Add asparagus, bell peppers and onion, and sauté for 5 to 10 minutes or until the vegetables begin to soften.

6. Add the spinach, and cook for 3 to 4 minutes, or until the spinach wilts.

7. Stir in the pesto until well-incorporated.

8. Pour the vegetable mixture into a bowl and set aside to cool.

9. In a small bowl, whisk the egg and set aside.

10. Using a brush, coat the bottom and sides of the loaf pan with olive oil.

11. Cut a piece of parchment paper into 15x10-inch piece. Place the piece of parchment paper inside of the loaf pan allowing the edges to overhang over the sides. Brush parchment paper with olive oil.

12. Place 1 sheet of puff pastry on the parchment paper. Press the puff pastry into the pan, being careful not to let the folds get caught in the parchment and allowing excess parchment and pastry to hang over sides. Brush the puff pastry with the beaten egg.

13. Cut 3 rectangles from the second puff pastry sheet. Press 2 of the puff pastry rectangles up against the short sides of the pan allowing the top to overhang from the edges. This pastry will end up being folded over the top of the mixture once the pan is filled.

14. Brush egg generously over the newly laid puff pastry.

15. Using a fork, prick the bottom (but not the sides) of the puff pastry.

16. Pour one-third of the vegetable mixture inside of the pastry mold.

17. Add carrot pieces, laying them end to end lengthwise in the pan until they are all used.

18. Add the remaining vegetable mixture and spread evenly throughout the pan.

19. Place the crumbled goat cheese over the vegetables inside of the puff pastry. Brush the edges with the beaten egg.

20. Place both pieces of overlapping puff pastry rectangles over the top of the vegetable mixture. Press to seal the edges.

21. Using cookie cutters, cut decorative leaves and/or designs from the remaining puff pastry. Press them on top of the Wellington and brush with egg.

22. Refrigerate for 30 minutes.

23. Place tomato sauce in a small saucepan and heat until warm. Keep on simmer until ready to serve.

24. Preheat the oven to 425F and place an oven rack on the second-lowest level. Brush the top of the Wellington with egg.

25. Bake for 15 minutes.

26. Reduce the oven heat to 350F and bake an additional 45 minutes more. Set aside to cool for 15 minutes.

27. Use parchment to lift the Wellington out of the loaf pan. Remove the parchment, and transfer the Wellington to flat serving platter.

28. Slice and serve with the warmed tomato sauce.

VEGAN BUTTERNUT ROAST

This butternut roast is stuffed with all the flavors of the season—from nuts to cranberries, lentils to fresh herbs—and is worthy of any holiday table.

SERVES 4 | PREP 25 MINS | COOK 1 HR 45 MINS

INGREDIENTS

1 large butternut squash, sliced in half, seeds removed

2 tablespoons olive oil plus extra for brushing the squash

1 medium red onion, diced

2 cloves garlic, peeled, minced

1/2 cup dry green lentils

1/2 cup fresh cranberries

2 sprigs fresh rosemary, leaves stripped, minced

2 sprigs fresh thyme, leaves stripped

1/2 teaspoon freshly grated nutmeg

2/3 cup red wine

2/3 cup vegetable stock

3 ounces fresh baby spinach, finely chopped

2 ounces pistachios, roughly chopped

INSTRUCTIONS

1. Preheat the oven to 350F.

2. Brush olive oil all over the flesh of the butternut squash halves.

3. Bake for up to 1 hour, depending upon size, or until the flesh is tender when pierced with a fork.

4. Remove the squash from the oven and set it aside until cool to the touch.

5. Heat the olive oil in a large skillet over low heat. Add the onion and garlic. Cook, stirring occasionally, for 5 minutes or until the onion is softened.

6. Add the lentils, cranberries, rosemary, thyme leaves, nutmeg, red wine and vegetable stock. Increase the heat to high and bring the mixture to the boil.

7. Cover the skillet with a lid and reduce the heat to low. Gently simmer the lentil mixture for about 30 minutes or until the liquid has evaporated. The lentils should be tender but not mushy.

8. Stir the spinach and pistachios into the lentil mixture until well combined. Transfer the mixture to a bowl and set aside.

9. Carefully scoop out most of the flesh from each of the halves of butternut squash, leaving a small amount of flesh all the way around the skin so that the squash holds its shape. Be careful not to tear the skin.

10. Transfer the squash to a large bowl. Use a potato masher to mash the squash. Add the lentil mixture and mix together.

11. Spoon the lentil mixture into each of the halves of the butternut squash.

12. Return the squash to the oven for 10 minutes to heat through.
13. Serve hot.

Sauces

Recipe by Jessica Gavin

HOMEMADE ORANGE CRANBERRY SAUCE

Planning a big feast? Making this cranberry sauce up to a week before the holiday allows the flavors to deepen and develop.

SERVES 16 | PREP 5 MINS | COOK 20 MINS

INGREDIENTS

12 ounces cranberries, washed

1/2 cup honey, or maple syrup

1/2 cup orange juice

1 teaspoon orange zest, freshly grated

1 cinnamon stick

INSTRUCTIONS

1. In a medium-sized pan add cranberries, honey, orange juice, zest and cinnamon stick.

2. Bring sauce to boil over medium-high heat. Reduce heat and simmer for 15 to 20 minutes or until cranberries pop and mixture has slightly thickened.

3. Make sure to stir occasionally, about every 5 minutes. Taste sauce and add more honey if desired.

4. Discard cinnamon stick and cool sauce.

5. The orange cranberry sauce can be stored in an airtight container refrigerated for up to 7 days.

VANILLA BOURBON BALSAMIC CRANBERRY SAUCE

Balsamic vinegar enhances cranberries' natural sweet-tart flavor, while vanilla and bourbon add warmth.

SERVES 8 | PREP 10 MINS | COOK 15 MINS | CHILL UNTIL COOL

INGREDIENTS

14 ounces fresh cranberries

3/4 cups sugar

1/2 cup water

1 tablespoon balsamic vinegar

2 tablespoons bourbon

1 tablespoon vanilla extract

INSTRUCTIONS

1. In large saucepan, combine all ingredients and mix well.

2. Bring mixture to boil. Reduce heat and simmer until cranberries burst and begin to break down and thicken, about 15 minutes. Occasionally stir well.

3. Remove from heat. Drain off 1/2 cup liquid and reserve for another use. Pour into jar or bowl, and allow to cool.

4. Refrigerate once cooled. Serve.

tip / Pour this cranberry sauce over baked Brie and serve with a sliced baguette for an unbelievably elegant appetizer.

CRUNCHY CRANBERRY SAUCE

This crunchy cranberry sauce grabs attention with vibrant flavors and a surprisingly addictive texture.

SERVES 10 | PREP 25 MINS | CHILL 2 HRS

INGREDIENTS

1 envelope (1/4 ounce) plain gelatin

1 cup plus 3 tablespoons of water, divided

3/4 cup granulated sugar

1 bag (12 ounces) fresh cranberries

1/2 tablespoon fresh lemon juice

1/4 teaspoon ground cinnamon

4 stalks celery, finely diced

1 medium apple, finely diced

1/2 cup walnut pieces

INSTRUCTIONS

1. In small bowl, stir gelatin into 3 tablespoons water. Allow mixture to sit until gelatin has absorbed water and formed thick jelly-like texture, about 5 minutes.

2. In medium saucepan, bring sugar and remaining 1 cup water to boil. Stir briefly to dissolve sugar, then add cranberries.

3. Return water to boil, then turn heat down to medium-low. Cover and simmer for about 10 minutes or until cranberries burst.

4. Stir in softened gelatin, lemon juice and cinnamon. Place saucepan in refrigerator to cool slightly.

5. In large bowl, combine celery, apple and walnuts.

6. Pour cranberry mixture into bowl with celery mixture. Stir to combine, then place cranberry sauce in refrigerator to cool completely, about 2 hours.

tip / Grate fresh orange or lemon zest over the finished dish for some contrasting color.

JALAPEÑO CRANBERRY SAUCE

Kick up your meal a notch with this zingy marriage of tart, sweet and spicy.

SERVES 8 | PREP 10 MINS | 15 MINS + COOL   DF EF GF GR NF VG

INGREDIENTS

3/4 cup water

3/4 cup sugar

2-3/4 cups whole cranberries, fresh or frozen

1 large or 2 small jalapeños, seeded, deveined and minced

INSTRUCTIONS

1. In medium saucepan over medium-high heat, bring water and sugar to boil.

2. Add cranberries and jalapeños; return to boil.

3. Reduce heat and simmer for 10 minutes, stirring occasionally.

4. Pour into bowl and cover. Cool completely at room temperature, then refrigerate until ready to serve.

tip / Always wear gloves when working with fresh hot peppers.

APPLE CRANBERRY SAUCE

SERVES 6 | PREP 10 MINS
COOK 10 MINS

INGREDIENTS

3/4 cup water

1 cup granulated sugar

1 Granny Smith apple, peeled and diced

3 cups whole cranberries, fresh or frozen

INSTRUCTIONS

1. Combine water and sugar in medium saucepan and bring to boil over medium-high heat. Add apples and cranberries, and return to boil. Reduce heat and simmer for 10 minutes, stirring occasionally.

2. Remove from heat and pour sauce into bowl. Cover and let cool at room temperature.

3. Refrigerate until ready to serve.

 tip / This cranberry sauce goes well with leftover chicken and pork, too.

CRANBERRY BACON GRAVY

SERVES 6 | PREP 10 MINS
COOK 40 MINS

INGREDIENTS

One bag (12 ounces) fresh frozen cranberries

3/4 cup white sugar

1 cup water

1/4 cup cornstarch

4 cups chicken broth

1/2 cup bacon bits

Salt and pepper, to taste

INSTRUCTIONS

1. In saucepan, cook cranberries and sugar over low heat, stirring constantly until sugar is dissolved and cranberries have burst.

2. In blender, purée mixture until smooth.

3. Bring cranberries to room temperature before adding them to other ingredients.

4. In saucepan over low heat, whisk cornstarch and chicken broth until smooth, 3 to 5 minutes.

5. Bring to boil. Add cranberries.

6. Boil gravy, whisking occasionally until reduced and thickened (20 to 25 minutes).

7. Stir in bacon bits, and season with salt and pepper. Keep warm until ready to serve.

BEST BASIC PAN GRAVY

This tried-and-true pan gravy is absolutely delicious, which is why it has stood the test of time.

SERVES 10–12 | PREP 10 MINS | COOK 15 MINS

INGREDIENTS

3 cups reduced-sodium chicken stock

1 cup red wine (optional)

1/3 cup all-purpose flour

1 tablespoon fresh herbs such as oregano, thyme and rosemary

Kosher salt

Freshly ground black pepper

INSTRUCTIONS

1. Remove turkey from roasting pan and set aside to rest before carving. Leave drippings in pan and place on burner over medium heat.

2. Add broth (and wine, if using). Whisk, making sure to scrape bottom of pan to loosen all turkey dripping bits.

3. Reduce mixture slightly by cooking for another 2 to 3 minutes.

4. Transfer liquid to fat separator and let sit for 5 minutes to allow fat to separate.

5. Return about 2/3 to 3/4 cup of fat to roasting pan and increase heat to medium-high.

6. Whisk in flour.

7. Whisk continuously for a few minutes until mixture starts to thicken and becomes smooth.

8. Gradually add liquid back to pan and whisk until smooth and of desired consistency, approximately 5 to 6 minutes.

9. Add herbs and whisk to combine.

10. Season with salt and pepper.

tip / Traditional gravy is best made right in the roasting pan after you remove the bird so you get every last bit of flavor. Bonus: One less pot to wash!

TURKEY-ONION GRAVY

Forego the pressure of making a complicated gravy and whip up this easy turkey-onion gravy instead.

SERVES 4–6 | PREP 10 MINS | COOK 18 MINS

INGREDIENTS

1-1/2 cups turkey drippings

2 tablespoons olive oil

2 medium onions, thinly sliced

1/2 cup all-purpose flour

2 cups chicken broth

Salt, to taste

Freshly ground pepper, to taste

2 tablespoons minced
fresh chives

INSTRUCTIONS

1. To get turkey drippings, transfer roasted turkey to serving platter to rest while you prepare other ingredients. Empty roasting pan, straining drippings. Set aside 1-1/2 cups drippings.

2. Heat olive oil in sauté pan over medium-high heat. Add onions and cook, stirring often, for 10 to 13 minutes, or until onions are lightly browned.

3. Sprinkle flour over onions and whisk until flour is dissolved.

4. Add chicken broth and reserved turkey drippings, whisking to combine.

5. Continuously whisk until gravy thickens. Reduce heat and simmer for 5 minutes.

6. Add salt and pepper to taste and whisk in minced chives.

7. Transfer gravy to gravy boat and serve hot.

LEMON-ROSEMARY TURKEY GRAVY

This thick, rich gravy gets its intense flavor from turkey broth, an infusion of citrus and the earthy essence of fresh rosemary.

SERVES 8–10 | PREP 5 MINS | COOK 10 MINS

INGREDIENTS

6 tablespoons cornstarch

1/4 cup cold water

3 cups turkey broth

1 teaspoon rosemary, minced

2 tablespoons fresh lemon juice

Salt and freshly ground
black pepper, to taste

INSTRUCTIONS

1. Whisk cornstarch into cold water in a small bowl. Set aside.

2. Pour turkey broth back into turkey roasting pan.

3. Set roasting pan on stovetop over medium-high heat.

4. Whisk cornstarch slurry into turkey broth. Add minced rosemary and lemon juice. Cook, stirring continuously, until gravy thickens.

5. Taste and season with salt and pepper.

 tip / The drippings from the turkey make a great turkey broth. Use a gravy separator to get as much of the turkey drippings from the roasting pan as possible.

Desserts

Recipe by Sally McKenney

DARK CHOCOLATE PECAN PIE

Sea salt cuts the sweetness of a pie that is traditionally extra-sugary, lending more fullness to the pecan and dark chocolate flavors.

MAKES 1 PIE | PREP 2 HRS 30 MINS | COOK 50 MINS

INGREDIENTS

Dough for 1 homemade pie crust, chilled

2-1/2 cups shelled pecans

1 cup dark chocolate chips

3 large eggs, at room temperature

1 cup dark corn syrup

1/2 cup packed dark brown sugar (or light brown)

1/4 cup unsalted butter, melted and slightly cooled

1-1/2 teaspoons pure vanilla extract

1/2 teaspoon sea salt

1/2 teaspoon ground cinnamon

Sea salt for topping

INSTRUCTIONS

1. Preheat oven to 350F.

2. On a floured work surface, roll out chilled dough. Turn the dough about a quarter turn after every few rolls until you have a circle 12 inches in diameter.

3. Carefully place the dough into a 9-inch pie dish. Tuck it in with your fingers, making sure it is smooth. Flute or crimp the edges of the crust.

4. Spread pecans evenly inside pie crust and sprinkle the chocolate chips evenly on top. Set aside.

5. Whisk the eggs, corn syrup, brown sugar, melted butter, vanilla, salt and cinnamon together in a large bowl. Once completely combined and thick, pour evenly over pecans and chocolate chips.

6. Bake the pie for 40 to 50 minutes, or until the top is lightly browned. After the first 20 minutes of bake time, place a pie crust shield on top of the pie to prevent the edges from browning too quickly. You can also tent a piece of aluminum foil over the whole pie if the top is browning too quickly. Remove finished pie from the oven and place on a wire rack to cool completely. The pie filling will set as it cools.

7. Slice and serve pie warm or at room temperature. Top with whipped cream and chocolate shavings, if desired. Cover and store leftover pie at room temperature for 1 to 2 days or in the refrigerator for 4 to 5 days.

Recipe by Sally McKenney

PEPPERMINT MOCHA COOKIES

These delightful holiday cookies have a secret ingredient—espresso powder. They'll be the star of any cookie exchange.

MAKES 20 COOKIES | PREP 15 MINS (PLUS CHILLING) | COOK 9 MINS

INGREDIENTS

1/2 cup unsalted butter, softened to room temperature

1/2 cup granulated sugar

1/2 cup packed light or dark brown sugar

1 large egg, at room temperature

1 teaspoon pure vanilla extract

1 teaspoon peppermint extract

1 cup all-purpose flour

1/2 cup + 2 tablespoons unsweetened natural cocoa powder

1 teaspoon baking soda

2 teaspoons espresso powder or 1 tablespoon instant coffee granules

1/8 teaspoon salt

1 cup mini or regular size semi-sweet chocolate chips

8 ounces white chocolate, coarsely chopped

3 large candy canes, crushed

INSTRUCTIONS

1. In a large bowl using a hand-held mixer or stand mixer fitted with a paddle attachment, beat the butter for 1 minute on medium speed until completely smooth and creamy. Add the granulated sugar and brown sugar and beat on medium high speed until fluffy and light in color. Beat in egg, vanilla and peppermint extracts on high speed. Scrape down the sides and bottom of the bowl as needed.

2. In a separate bowl, whisk the flour, cocoa powder, baking soda, espresso powder, and salt together until combined. On low speed, slowly mix into the wet ingredients until combined. The cookie dough will be quite thick. Switch to high speed and beat in the chocolate chips. The cookie dough will be sticky. Cover dough tightly with aluminum foil or plastic wrap and chill for at least 3 hours and up to 3 days. Chilling is mandatory for this cookie dough. I always chill mine overnight.

3. Remove cookie dough from the refrigerator and allow to sit at room temperature for 20 minutes-- if the cookie dough chilled longer than 3 hours, let it sit at room temperature for about 30 minutes. This makes the cookie dough easier to scoop and roll.

4. Preheat oven to 350F.

5. Line two large baking sheets with parchment paper or silicone baking mats. Set aside.

6. Scoop and roll balls of dough, about 1.5 tablespoons of dough each, into balls and place on the baking sheets.

7. Bake the cookies for 8 to 9 minutes. Rotate the pans once during baking. The baked cookies will look extremely soft in the centers when you remove them from the oven. Allow to cool for 5 minutes on the cookie sheet. They will slightly deflate as you let them cool. Transfer to cooling rack to cool completely.

8. Melt the chopped white chocolate in a double boiler or carefully use the microwave. For the microwave, place the white chocolate in a medium heat-proof bowl. Melt in 15 second increments, stirring after each increment until completely melted and smooth. Dip each completely cooled cookie halfway into the white chocolate and place onto a parchment or silicone baking mat-lined baking sheet. Sprinkle crushed candy canes on top of the chocolate. Place the baking sheet into the refrigerator to help the chocolate set.

photo by Sally McKenney

Recipe by Monique Kilgore

SWEET POTATO PIE

An alternative to traditional pumpkin pie, this sweet potato pie is made with roasted sweet potatoes, a splash of pineapple juice and the secret ingredient: browned butter.

MAKES 1 PIE | PREP 60 MINS | COOK 55 MINS

INGREDIENTS

1 9-inch pie crust

1/2 cup unsalted butter, cut into cubes or slices

2 pounds sweet potatoes, washed and dried (about 2 cups pureed)

1/2 cup light brown sugar, packed

1/2 cup granulated sugar

1/2 cup evaporated milk

2 eggs, room temperature

1 teaspoon vanilla extract

1/2 teaspoon cinnamon

1/2 teaspoon nutmeg

1/4 teaspoon ginger

Tiny pinch cloves (optional)

2 tablespoons orange or pineapple juice

1 1/2 tablespoons flour

INSTRUCTIONS

1. Preheat oven to 425F.

2. Pierce sweet potatoes with a fork several times.

3. Place on foil-lined baking sheet.

4. Bake for 45 minutes or until very tender.

5. Let cool while preparing the brown butter.

6. To make the brown butter, add butter to a heavy-bottom skillet over medium heat.

7. Once butter has melted it will begin to foam a bit, whisk continuously while scraping the bottom of the pan.

8. The butter will begin to turn golden and form golden brown bits on the bottom of the pan, keep whisking.

9. Once the aromas become nutty (almost like the smell of caramel) and the solids in the bottom of the pan are golden brown remove from heat.

10. Pour into a glass dish (including the brown solids) and set aside to let cool.

11. In a large bowl, scoop out the flesh of the cooled sweet potatoes.

12. Mix until creamy and smooth, adding a few splashes of water (or milk) until you have the texture of a very thick puree.

13. Mix in the cooled brown butter until smooth.

14. Mix in the brown sugar, white sugar, evaporated milk, eggs, vanilla extract, cinnamon, nutmeg, ginger, clove (if using), juice and flour until well combined.

15. Pour into pie crust shell and smooth the top.

16. Bake on middle rack in preheated 350F oven for 55 minutes.

17. Remove from oven and let cool completely until the middle is firmly set.

18. Refrigerate until ready to serve.

19. Serve with sweetened whipped cream or vanilla ice cream.

Recipe by Monique Kilgore

RED VELVET CREAM CHEESE COOKIE SANDWICHES

Bring festive color to your dessert spread with these soft and chewy red velvet cookies.

MAKES 16 SANDWICHES | PREP 8 MINS | COOK 8 MINS

INGREDIENTS

Cookies

1 cup granulated sugar

1/2 cup unsalted butter, room temperature

1 egg

2 tablespoons buttermilk

1/2 teaspoon vanilla extract

2 tablespoons red food coloring

1 1/2 cups all-purpose flour

1/2 teaspoon baking soda

1/2 teaspoon salt

2 tablespoons unsweetened cocoa powder

Cream cheese filling

8 ounces cream cheese

1 cup powdered sugar

1/4 cup butter, room temperature

1/2 teaspoon vanilla extract

INSTRUCTIONS

1. Preheat oven to 350F.

2. Line a baking pan with parchment paper, set aside

3. In a large bowl cream together sugar and butter.

4. Mix in egg, buttermilk and vanilla extract.

5. Stir in red food coloring. Set aside.

6. In a separate bowl, whisk together flour, baking soda, salt and unsweetened cocoa powder.

7. Stir dry ingredients into the wet ingredients just until combined.

8. Using a mini ice cream scoop, scoop out the dough and place 2 inches apart on a baking sheet. Roll the balls to make them smoother on the surface.

9. Bake for 7 to 8 minutes.

10. Remove from oven and let cookies sit in the pan for 1 to 2 minutes and then place on a cooling rack.

11. To make the cream cheese filling, cream together cream cheese, powdered sugar, butter and vanilla extract until combined.

12. Place filling in a piping bag.

13. Once cookies are cooled, pipe cream cheese filling in the center of a cookie and top with another cookie.

14. Place in the fridge for at least 3 hours to set the filling.

15. Store in the fridge.

Recipe by Katie Higgins

BLACK BEAN BROWNIES

These rich brownies are so much like the real thing, no one will guess they're actually made with beans instead of flour.

MAKES 12 | PREP 5 MINS | COOK 15 MINS

INGREDIENTS

1 1/2 cups black beans (15-ounce can, drained and rinsed very well)

2 tablespoons cocoa powder

1/2 cup quick oats

1/4 teaspoon salt

1/3 cup pure maple syrup, honey, or agave

Pinch uncut stevia OR 2 tablespoons sugar (or omit and increase maple syrup to 1/2 cup)

1/4 cup coconut or vegetable oil

2 teaspoons pure vanilla extract

1/2 teaspoon baking powder

1/2 cup to 2/3 cup chocolate chips

More chips, for presentation (optional)

INSTRUCTIONS

1. Preheat oven to 350F.

2. Combine all ingredients except chips in a food processor, and blend until completely smooth.

3. Stir in the chips, then pour into a greased 8×8 pan.

4. Optional: Sprinkle extra chocolate chips over the top.

5. Bake 15 to 18 minutes, then let cool at least 10 minutes before cutting. If brownies still look a bit undercooked, refrigerate overnight and they will firm up.

HOLIDAY MIXED FRUIT PIE

The best way to bring sweet, tart berries to the table is with this mixed fruit pie, perfect for the holidays.

SERVES 8 | PREP 30 MINS PLUS TIME TO CHILL CRUST | COOK 45 MINS PLUS 15-30 MINS COOLING

INGREDIENTS

Crust

Dough for three 9-inch pie crusts, one rolled into a 12-inch circle, the remainder rolled and cut into 60 mini decorative leaves

Filling

5 cups mixed fruit: equal amounts blackberries and raspberries and slightly fewer cranberries, plus a handful of fresh berries for garnish

3/4 cups, plus 2 tablespoons sugar, divided

1 teaspoon fresh lemon juice

1/2 teaspoons lemon zest

Pinch of fresh nutmeg

2 tablespoons instant quick-cooking tapioca

1/2 teaspoon salt

1 tablespoon unsalted butter, cut into small pieces

2 egg whites

2 tablespoons water

Powdered sugar for garnish

INSTRUCTIONS

1. Place one of the rolled-out pieces of pie dough into a 9-inch pie pan and gently flute the edges onto the edge of the pie plate. Cover with plastic wrap and refrigerate until well chilled.

2. Preheat oven to 425F.

3. Place a piece of parchment paper on a baking tray. Place tray on lower rack of oven.

4. Place berries, 3/4 cup sugar, lemon juice, lemon zest, nutmeg, tapioca and salt into a bowl.

5. Mash the mixture gently, but leave most berries whole. Stir to combine ingredients. Pour filling into the chilled crust.

6. Dot filling with pieces of butter; set aside.

7. In a small bowl, whisk egg whites with water together until well combined. Set aside.

8. Brush the bottom center of each cut-out pastry leaf with egg wash before placing on edge of crust. Place one row of leaves on the outside edge of the pie spaced close together.

9. Place the remaining leaves on a parchment lined baking sheet.

10. Brush crust and leaves with egg wash mixture. Repeat process with remaining leaves on the baking tray.

11. Place pie and tray of leaves in the oven, with the pie on the middle rack.

12. Remove tray of leaves when slightly browned, about 7 minutes total baking time. Set aside.

13. After 15 minutes of baking time for the pie, when the crust is just golden, reduce heat to 350F. Bake pie until golden brown and bubbling, about 30 minutes more. If top leaves become too brown,

cover the pastry edges with aluminum foil.

14. Remove pie and place on cooling rack.

15. While the pie is still hot, immediately arrange additional leaves on top of the first row of leaves.

16. Allow pie to cool completely.

17. Add a small number of fresh berries to center of pie.

18. Lightly dust leaves and fresh berries with confectioners sugar.

19. Slice and serve.

SKILLET APPLE PIE

Every bite of this delish dessert is full of cinnamon-spiced, sugar-sweet chunks of apples nestled between two crispy crusts, baked to bubbly goodness.

SERVES 8 | PREP 45 MINS | BAKE 60 MINS

INGREDIENTS

5 Granny Smith apples, peeled, cored and chopped

5 Golden Delicious apples, peeled, cored and chopped

3 tablespoons cornstarch

1 teaspoon ground cinnamon

3/4 cup granulated sugar

8 tablespoons unsalted butter

1 cup light brown sugar

1 package refrigerated pie crusts (or 2 frozen pie crusts, defrosted), rolled into pie rounds

1 egg white

1 tablespoon water

2 tablespoons granulated sugar

INSTRUCTIONS

1. Preheat oven to 350F.
2. Toss chopped apples in cornstarch, cinnamon and 3/4 cup granulated sugar.
3. Melt butter in skillet.
4. Add brown sugar and heat until dissolved.
5. Remove skillet from heat and place one pie crust in bottom of skillet.
6. Bake crust for nine minutes.
7. Drain apple mixture. Add into pie.
8. Top with remaining pie crust.
9. Whisk egg white to foamy consistency.
10. Add water and mix well.
11. Brush mixture across top of crust.
12. Sprinkle remaining granulated sugar across top of pie.
13. Cut several slits in top for steam to escape.
14. Bake for 60 minutes, until crust is golden-brown.

tip / Instead of the usual pie made in a pie pan, try baking your apple pie in a cast-iron skillet.

VEGAN CHOCOLATE PECAN PIE

This recipe lets you eat clean while enjoying a quintessential Southern dessert: pecan pie.

SERVES 6-8 | PREP 20 MINS | COOK 45 MINS

INGREDIENTS

2 teaspoons vanilla extract

1/4 teaspoon salt

2 teaspoons cornstarch

1/2 cup pure maple syrup

1 tablespoon sugar

12.3 ounces silken firm tofu

2 tablespoons molasses

2 tablespoons cocoa powder

1 cup raw pecans, chopped; plus 60 whole pecans for garnish

1 premade graham cracker pie crust

INSTRUCTIONS

1. Preheat oven to 350F.

2. Place vanilla, salt, cornstarch, maple syrup, sugar, tofu, molasses and cocoa powder in a blender or food processor. Blend until very smooth.

3. Add the pecans and pulse once.

4. Pour the filling into a prepared pie crust and top with whole pecans arranged in three circles.

5. Bake 45 minutes.

6. Remove from oven, let cool completely, then place in refrigerator to chill.

7. Once chilled, slice and serve with whipped cream.

VEGAN WHIPPED CREAM

This easy vegan whipped cream is just as rich and creamy as the original, thanks to coconut cream.

MAKES 1 CUP | PREP 8 MINS

INGREDIENTS

1 can coconut cream, refrigerated

2 tablespoons powdered sugar, or more to taste

1 teaspoon vanilla

INSTRUCTIONS

1. Open the can of coconut cream and scoop the thick creamy part into a large bowl. Set aside the liquid for another recipe.

2. Note: Coconut cream should be super-thick. If not, place the can in the refrigerator overnight.

3. Using a handheld mixer, whip the cream, adding in sweetener and vanilla until stiff peaks are reached.

4. Serve immediately.

tip / Coconut cream is different from coconut milk because it contains less water and is much thicker.

CRANBERRY ALMOND PIE

This luscious pie offers a combination of apples and cranberries on top of an almond-flavored crust for a warming, seasonal dessert.

SERVES 8-10 | PIE CRUST PREP 30 MINS, CHILL 2 HRS | PIE PREP 40 MINS, BAKE 55 MINS

INGREDIENTS

Crust

2-1/2 cups all-purpose flour

1-1/4 teaspoons salt

6 tablespoons unsalted butter, chilled and cubed

3/4 cup vegetable shortening, chilled

1/2 cup ice water

Filling

4 large apples, cored, peeled and sliced into 1/2-inch slices (about 7-8 cups)

1 cup fresh or frozen cranberries (do not thaw)

1/2 cup granulated sugar

2 tablespoons cornstarch

2 teaspoons ground cinnamon

1/4 teaspoon ground cloves

1/4 teaspoon ground nutmeg

7 ounces almond paste

2 tablespoons unsalted butter, cold and cubed

Egg wash: 1 large egg beaten with 1 tablespoon milk

Coarse sugar for sprinkling (optional)

INSTRUCTIONS

Make the crust

1. Mix the flour and salt together in a large bowl. Add the butter and shortening.

2. Using a pastry cutter or two forks, cut the butter and shortening into the flour mixture until it resembles coarse meal (pea-sized bits with a few larger bits of fat is okay). A pastry cutter makes this step easy and quick.

3. Measure 1/2 cup water and add ice. Stir it around. From that, measure 1/2 cup water—since the ice has melted a bit.

4. Drizzle the cold water into the flour mixture, one tablespoon at a time. Stir with a rubber spatula or wooden spoon after every tablespoon. Stop adding water when the dough begins to form large clumps; do not add any more water than you need to. In a drier climate or during winter months, you may need a little more water to bring the dough together.

5. Transfer the pie dough to a floured work surface. The dough should come together easily and should not feel overly sticky. Using floured hands, fold the dough into itself until the flour is fully incorporated into the fats. Form it into a ball. Divide dough in half. Flatten each half into 1-inch-thick rounds using your hands.

6. Wrap each round tightly in plastic wrap. Refrigerate for at least two hours, or up to five days.

Make the filling and prep pie

1. Preheat oven to 400F.

2. Stir apples, cranberries, granulated sugar, cornstarch, cinnamon, cloves and nutmeg together in a large bowl. Set filling aside as the oven preheats.

3. On a floured work surface, roll out one of the rounds of chilled dough (keep the other in the refrigerator). Turn the dough about a quarter turn after every few rolls until you have a circle 12 inches in diameter. Carefully place the dough into a 9x2-inch pie dish. Tuck it in with your fingers, making sure it is smooth.

4. Unwrap the almond paste. Flatten it out into a 9-inch disc to fit snug into the bottom of the pie. Place on top of the pie crust. Spoon the filling on top of the almond paste, leaving any excess liquid in the bowl. Dot the pieces of butter on top of the filling. Place the pie in the refrigerator until ready to arrange the lattice.

5. To make the lattice, remove the other round of chilled pie dough from the refrigerator. Roll the dough into a circle 12 inches in diameter. Using a sharp knife or pizza cutter, cut 24 1/2-inch strips. Remove the pie from the refrigerator and carefully thread the pie dough strips over and under one another to create the lattice, pulling back strips as necessary to weave. Press the edges of the strips into the bottom pie crust edges to seal. Use a small knife to trim off excess dough. Flute the edges or crimp with a fork. With any leftover dough, cut into fall-inspired shapes and place on top of the lattice. (Alternatively, you can simply cover the filling with the 12-inch pie dough circle. Cut slits in the top to form steam vents. Trim and crimp the edges.)

6. Lightly brush the top of the pie crust with the egg wash and sprinkle with coarse sugar, if desired.

7. Place the pie onto a large baking sheet and bake for 20 minutes. After the first 20 minutes of bake time, place a pie crust shield or tin foil tent on top of the pie to prevent the edges from browning too quickly. Keeping the pie in the oven, turn the temperature down to 350F and bake for an additional 30 to 35 minutes.

8. Allow the pie to cool for three full hours at room temperature before serving. This resting time allows the filling to thicken. Cover leftovers tightly and store in the refrigerator for up to five days.

GRAIN-FREE PECAN PIE

A classic fall flavor, this pecan pie takes a contemporary gluten-free and grain-free approach.

SERVES 8 | PREP 50 MINS | COOK 60 MINS

INGREDIENTS

Crust

3/4 cup almond flour

1/3 cup coconut flour

1/2 cup coconut oil

1/4 teaspoon gluten-free vanilla extract

2 tablespoons Swerve confectioners sugar

1/4 teaspoon salt

1 large egg

Filling

1 cup unsalted butter

1 cup Swerve confectioners sugar

1 cup unsweetened full-fat coconut milk

3 eggs, beaten

2 teaspoons gluten-free vanilla extract

1/2 teaspoon unsulfured molasses

1/4 teaspoon sea salt

2 cups pecan halves (1 cup chopped, 1 cup for topping)

INSTRUCTIONS

Crust

1. Preheat oven to 325F.

2. Grease a 9-inch or 9-1/2-inch pie pan.

3. In medium bowl, mix almond flour, coconut flour, coconut oil, vanilla, sugar and salt. Add egg and mix until well-combined.

4. Press dough into bottom and up sides of pie pan.

5. Press sides of crust with fork tines to make design.

6. Prebake crust for 15 minutes, or until set.

Filling

1. Heat butter on high heat in enameled cast-iron or heavy-bottomed saucepan that holds 2–3 quarts, whisking constantly to make sure butter heats evenly.

2. When butter starts boiling, watch for brown streaks or flecks at bottom of the pan as you whisk. Remove it from heat immediately to prevent burning.

3. Add sugar and coconut milk to pan and whisk until smooth. Let sauce cool in pan, whisking every 5 minutes. Do not allow it to settle.

4. In medium bowl, beat eggs with cooled syrup, vanilla, salt, molasses and chopped pecans.

5. Pour mixture into crust and top with remaining cup of whole pecans in design of your liking.

6. Bake at 325F for 40 to 45 minutes or until set. Cover edges of pie with aluminum foil to prevent burning.

PUMPKIN CHEESECAKE PARFAITS

These parfaits combine creamy pumpkin, rich cheesecake and a crunchy graham cracker crust for a delicious blend of fall flavors.

SERVES 6-8 | PREP 15 MINS | ASSEMBLE 15 MINS

INGREDIENTS

1 cup graham cracker crumbs

4 tablespoons butter, melted

1 (15-ounce) can of pumpkin puree

1 (8-ounce) package cream cheese

1/3 cup brown sugar

1 teaspoon vanilla extract

3 teaspoons pumpkin pie spice

6 ounces whipped topping

1 can whipped cream

INSTRUCTIONS

1. In a medium bowl, combine graham cracker crumbs and melted butter. Divide the crumbs evenly among parfait the glasses, gently pressing into the bottom of each glass to form a crust.

2. In a large bowl, beat pumpkin puree, cream cheese, brown sugar, vanilla and pumpkin pie spice until smooth and creamy. Using a spatula, gently fold in whipped topping until combined.

3. To assemble parfaits, spoon a thick layer of the pumpkin cheesecake mixture on top of the graham cracker crust. Then layer a thin swirl of whipped cream. Next add another thick layer of pumpkin cheesecake mixture. Finish with a swirl of whipped cream and a sprinkle of graham cracker crumbs.

4. Refrigerate until ready to serve.

tip / If you don't have enough parfait glasses, this is also spectacular as one giant trifle.

NO-BAKE PUMPKIN PIE

Get all of fall's best flavors in a light and airy dessert that's ready in less than 30 minutes.

SERVES 12 | PREP 10 MINS | SET 20 MINS

INGREDIENTS

1/2 cup whole milk

1 large box (6 serving size)
vanilla bean pudding mix

2 teaspoons pumpkin pie spice

1 teaspoon vanilla bean paste

1 cup pumpkin puree

1 (8-ounce) container
whipped topping

12 mini graham cracker pie crusts

Whipped cream, for serving

INSTRUCTIONS

1. In a large bowl whisk together whole milk and dry pudding mix. Add in pumpkin pie spice, vanilla bean paste and pumpkin puree. Whisk to combine.

2. Fold in whipped topping until completely combined and mixture is smooth.

3. Spoon into crusts and let sit for at least 20 minutes before serving.

4. Serve topped with whipped cream if desired.

PUMPKIN PIE WITH HARVEST-SPICED CREAM AND CARAMELIZED ALMONDS

This classic pumpkin pie is given a seasonal twist with a spiced whipped cream and a sweet almond crunch.

SERVES 8 | PREP 25 MINS | COOK 1 HR AND 3 MINS

INGREDIENTS

1 pre-made pie crust

2 large eggs, beaten

14-ounce can sweetened condensed milk

15-ounce can pumpkin

1/4 cup firmly-packed brown sugar

1 teaspoon pumpkin pie spice

1/2 teaspoon nutmeg

1 teaspoon vanilla extract

For the spiced whipped cream

1/2 cup sour cream

2 tablespoons brown sugar

1/4 teaspoon pumpkin pie spice

1/4 cup whipping cream

For the caramelized almonds

1/2 cup slivered almonds

1/4 cup sugar

INSTRUCTIONS

Pumpkin pie

1. Preheat oven to 450F.

2. Fit pie crust into a 9-inch pie plate. Fold edges under and crimp. Prick bottom and sides of pie crust with a knife.

3. Bake pie crust for 8 minutes. Remove and allow pie shell to cool.

4. In a large bowl, combine eggs, condensed milk, pumpkin, brown sugar, pie spice, nutmeg and vanilla together. Mix well.

5. Pour mixture into the pie crust. Bake at 350F for 50-55 minutes, or until a knife inserted comes out clean.

6. Cool.

7. Serve with a dollop of spiced whipped cream and a sprinkling of caramelized almonds.

Spiced whipped cream

1. Combine the sour cream, brown sugar and pumpkin pie spice in a small bowl. Allow to set at room temperature for 5 minutes.

2. Whisk in the whipped cream. Once combined well, cover and place in refrigerator.

Caramelized almonds

1. Combine almonds with sugar in large skillet.

2. Cook over low heat, stirring constantly until the sugar has melted and the almonds are light brown in color.

3. Remove from pan, spreading on a large baking sheet.

4. Allow to cool, then break into small pieces. Set aside until ready to use.

PRESSURE COOKER SALTED CARAMEL CHEESECAKE

Velvety, rich and delicious, few desserts rule the table like cheesecake. Preparing it in your pressure cooker takes half the time—and the result is dense, creamy and delicious.

SERVES 12 | PREP 22 MINS | COOK 48 MINS

INGREDIENTS

28 graham crackers, crushed

1/4 cup white sugar

1/2 cup unsalted butter, melted

16 ounces cream cheese, room temperature

1/2 cup light brown sugar

1/4 cup sour cream

1 tablespoon flour

1/2 teaspoon kosher salt

1-1/2 teaspoons vanilla

2 eggs

Topping

1/2 cup caramel sauce

1 teaspoon flaked sea salt

INSTRUCTIONS

1. Spray a 7-inch springform pan lightly with cooking spray.

2. Cut a piece of parchment paper in a circle to fit the bottom of the pan, then spray with cooking spray.

3. In a large bowl, combine the graham crackers, white sugar and butter. Mix well.

4. Press the mixture firmly into the bottom and up the sides of the prepared pan.

5. Bake at 350F for 13 minutes. Remove and set aside.

6. In the bowl of a stand mixer, blend the cream cheese and sugar until well combined.

7. Add the sour cream and mix until smooth.

8. Add the flour, salt and vanilla, scraping the sides of the bowl as necessary.

9. Add in the eggs, then mix again until just smooth. At this stage, don't overmix the batter.

10. Pour the cream cheese mixture into the prepared crust.

11. Pour two cups of water into the bottom of the pressure cooker. Place the trivet that came with the pot into the bottom. Cut a piece of aluminum foil the same size as a paper towel. Place the foil under the paper towel, then put the springform pan on top of the paper towel. Wrap the bottom of the pan in the foil, using the paper towel as a barrier.

12. Next, take another piece of foil about 18 inches long and folded into thirds lengthwise. Place this under the springform pan and use the two sides as a sling to place the cheesecake into the pot. It will also make it easy to remove the cheesecake from the pressure cooker when it's done.

13. Once the pan is in the pressure cooker, secure the lid and select "Manual."

14. Adjust the pressure to high and set for 35 minutes, ensuring that the vent valve is in the closed position.

15. When cooking time is finished, allow the pressure to release naturally.

16. Remove the cheesecake from the pot using the sling you prepared and place on a wire rack to cool the cheesecake for one hour.

17. Cover the cheesecake in the pan with foil and place in the refrigerator to chill for at least four hours, or overnight.

18. When ready to serve, top the cheesecake with the caramel sauce and sprinkle with sea salt.

19. Using a butter knife, loosen the sides of the cheesecake from the pan and release the sides of the pan.

20. Store airtight in the refrigerator for up to 5 days.

HOLIDAY CHEESE TART WITH STRAWBERRY GLAZE

This eye-catching dessert is similar to a cheesecake but baked as a tart instead of in a springform pan.

SERVES 8 | PREP 40 MINS | COOK 50 MINS

INGREDIENTS

Crust

1/3 cup unsalted butter, melted

1 to 1-1/4 cups crushed graham crackers

Filling

16 ounces cream cheese, softened

3/4 cup granulated sugar

4 eggs

1 cup heavy cream

Strawberry glaze

1/2 cup thick strawberry jam

1 tablespoon hot water

4 ounces strawberries

2 ounces blackberries

2 ounces raspberries

1 ounce red or black currants

Fresh mint leaves, garnish

INSTRUCTIONS

1. Preheat oven to 350F.

2. Place the graham cracker crumbs in a bowl. Add the melted butter and mix well.

3. Evenly press the graham cracker mixture into the bottom and sides of a 12-inch tart pan.

4. Place the pan in the freezer for 15 to 20 minutes to firm up the crust.

5. Place the softened cream cheese in the mixing bowl of a stand mixer fitted with the paddle attachment. Beat the cream cheese until light and fluffy.

6. Slowly add the sugar to the cream cheese, continuously beating until well-combined.

7. Add the eggs one at a time and beat until fully incorporated.

8. Pour in the heavy cream. With the mixer on low to medium-low, gently blend until well-incorporated.

9. Pour the cream cheese filling into the crust-lined pan. The filling will be very high in the tart pan.

10. Place the tart pan on a parchment-lined baking sheet. Place the baking sheet in the oven and bake tart 40 to 50 minutes or until the edges are firm and the center still jiggles slightly.

11. Cool the tart at room temperature for one hour. Refrigerate for several more hours to set up the filling.

12. While the tart is baking, make the strawberry glaze. Combine the strawberry jam and hot water in the bowl of a food processor or blender and process until smooth.

13. Pour the strawberry glaze into a plastic bottle with a tip. Chill in the refrigerator until needed to decorate the cheese tart.

14. Once the cheese tart is chilled, decorate one-half with fresh strawberries, raspberries, blackberries and currants.

15. Using the strawberry glaze, pipe various sizes of dots onto the other half of the cheese tart in your preferred design.

16. Garnish the tart with fresh mint leaves.

17. Serve with an extra drizzle of strawberry glaze.

INGREDIENTS

2-1/2 cups all purpose flour

1/2 teaspoon salt

8 tablespoons rendered leaf lard,
cut into small pieces*

8 tablespoons unsalted butter,
cut into small pieces**

1/2 cup ice water plus 1-2
tablespoons more, as needed

Additional flour for rolling out the dough

TRADITIONAL PIE CRUST

Turn your favorite pie into a standout with this traditional pie crust recipe.

MAKES 2 (9-INCH) CRUSTS | PREP 1 HR AND 30 MINS (INCLUDING 1 HR OF CHILLING)

INSTRUCTIONS

1. Place the flour, salt, butter and lard** in the bowl of a food processor. Pulse 20 times.

2. Sprinkle ice cold water over the mixture and pulse again, 15 times.

3. Squeeze a handful of dough to see if it holds together. Add more water if necessary.

4. Divide the dough in half and make equal-size rounds about five inches across.

5. Wrap the rounds separately in plastic wrap. Chill for one hour.

6. Remove the dough from the refrigerator and allow to warm up slightly until the dough is soft to touch and easy to roll out.

7. Place one round on a floured pastry mat or board. Remove plastic wrap.

8. Sprinkle some flour on top of round. Roll your rolling pin from the center out in all directions. Do not use a back and forth motion.

9. When the dough is one to two inches larger than the pie pan, brush off extra flour.

10. Fold the dough in half and lay it in the pie pan carefully.

11. Push down into the pan to fit snugly. If it tears, add a little water and a small amount of flour pressed over the area to repair.

12. Add the pie filling.

13. If making a double crust pie, roll out the second dough in the same way and use it as the top crust.

Recipe notes

*Rendered leaf lard can be purchased from speciality butcher shops. If only unrendered leaf lard is available, you can render it by placing cubed pieces (approximately two inches in diameter) in a shallow pan in the oven or electric skillet and cooking on low heat at 250F for several hours until it melts. Strain through a cheesecloth and a strainer and place in container in refrigerator until it sets up. Divide and weigh leaf lard into equal portions of four ounces each. Wrap and chill or freeze until ready to use. The rendered lard will last three months in the freezer.

**14 ounces of butter can be substituted for the lard-butter combination.

GLUTEN-FREE, VEGAN GROUND NUT PIE CRUST

Instead of the typical ingredients found in a pie crust—like wheat flour and butter—this recipe uses plant-based, grain-free ingredients that still bring heaps of flavor.

MAKES 1 9-INCH PIE CRUST | PREP 15 MINS | COOK 20 MINS   (DF) (EF) (GF) (GR) (VG)

INGREDIENTS

1-1/2 teaspoons coconut oil, melted

1/2 teaspoon maple syrup

1/2 teaspoon vanilla

1/8 teaspoon ground nutmeg

4 tablespoons brown sugar

1 tablespoon water

2 cups pecans, whole or pieces

INSTRUCTIONS

1. Preheat oven to 325F.

2. In a small bowl, mix together the coconut oil and maple syrup. Whisk in brown sugar, vanilla, nutmeg and water.

3. Place pecans in food processor and pulse until finely ground.

4. Pour maple and sugar mixture into the food processor with the pecans. Continue processing until mixture begins falling from sides of bowl. Scrape down once.

5. Press mixture evenly into 9-inch glass pie pan.

6. Bake for 20 minutes or until lightly browned.

7. Remove from oven.

8. Allow to cool before using.

tip / Food processors are the easiest way to get finely ground pecans without hassle.

photo by Lola Hunt

INGREDIENTS

Cookies

1 cup unsalted butter at room temperature

3/4 cup vegetable oil

1-1/4 cups sugar

3/4 cup powdered sugar

2 tablespoons water

2 eggs

1/2 teaspoon baking soda

1/2 teaspoon cream of tartar

1 teaspoon salt

5-1/2 cups unbleached flour

Frosting

1/2 cup butter at room temperature

3/4 cup sour cream

4-1/2 cups powdered sugar

1/4 cup milk

1 teaspoon vanilla (or extract of your choice)

Food coloring

SODA SHOPPE SUGAR COOKIES

Sour cream brings a delicious tanginess to this special recipe—sure to be a favorite at all the holiday cookie swaps.

MAKES 3 DOZEN | PREP 30 MINS | BAKE 8 MINS

INSTRUCTIONS

Cookies

1. Preheat oven to 350F.

2. Cream butter, vegetable oil, sugars, water and eggs.

3. Combine dry ingredients. Mix well.

4. Slowly add dry ingredients to creamed ingredients.

5. Mix on with beaters on low setting until combined. Dough will be crumbly but should not be sticky. Do not overmix.

6. Using cookie scoop to keep size uniform, roll balls of cookie dough onto parchment-lined baking sheet. Allow plenty of space between each cookie.

7. Place about 1/4 cup sugar in bowl. Dip a small circular object (such as a juice glass) into sugar then firmly press it onto cookie ball to form lip around dough's edge.

8. Bake about eight minutes. If you are baking multiple sheets at once, they may need more time. Cookies should be just lightly browned on bottom. Do not overcook.

9. Cookies will be soft when they come out of the oven. Let them cool a few minutes on the sheet before moving to a cooling rack. Store unfrosted cookies in the fridge.

Frosting

1. Cream together butter and sour cream.

2. Very slowly add powdered sugar a little at a time until frosting is almost too thick to spread, then add dash of milk. Alternate adding powdered sugar and milk until frosting reaches desired consistency. Add extra powdered sugar and milk if needed.

3. Add several drops of food coloring and mix on high until fully incorporated.

4. Frost cookies right before serving.

CHOCOLATE-KAHLUA SNOWBALL COOKIES

Combining the sweetness of chocolate with the coffee flavor of Kahlua (and actual instant coffee granules) makes a no-bake cookie that caters to the grown-up palate.

MAKES 4 DOZEN | PREP 20 MINS

INGREDIENTS

1/3 cup Kahlua coffee liqueur

2 tablespoons light corn syrup

1 teaspoon instant coffee granules

1 (9-ounce) package chocolate wafer cookies, finely crushed

1/4 cup sifted powdered sugar

3/4 cup almonds, toasted and chopped

Additional powdered sugar

INSTRUCTIONS

1. In medium bowl, mix Kahlua, corn syrup and instant coffee granules until well blended.

2. In medium bowl, combine cookie crumbs, powdered sugar and almonds. Mix well.

3. Pour coffee mixture over crumb mixture, blending well.

4. Shape dough into 1-inch balls.

5. Roll each ball in powdered sugar 2 times, making sure to coat each cookie well.

6. Cookies can be stored in an airtight covered container for up to 1 week.

tip / These cookies are for the 21 and over crowd. They contain alcohol that does not get cooked out.

NO-BAKE COCONUT DATE BALLS

It's a good thing they are so easy to make—only five ingredients and no baking required—because they'll quickly disappear from your dessert table.

SERVES 12-16 | PREP 25 MINS

INGREDIENTS

1 cup sugar

1/2 cup unsalted butter

1 egg

1 (8-ounce) package
of dates, diced

2 cups crispy rice cereal

2 cups shredded coconut

INSTRUCTIONS

1. In a medium saucepan, over medium-low heat, combine sugar, butter, dates and the egg.

2. Heat for 7-8 minutes, stirring often.

3. In a large bowl, pour mixture over crispy rice cereal and allow to cool.

4. Form mixture into balls and roll in coconut.

Photo by Betsy Bailey

TRUFFLES THREE WAYS

This chocolate truffle recipe is a deceptively simple way to make nearly 80 truffles rolled in a tasty trio of coatings.

MAKES 76 TRUFFLES | PREP 1 HR 45 MINS | CHILL 1 HOUR

INGREDIENTS

14 ounces, good-quality bittersweet bar chocolate (at least 60% cocoa), cut into 1/4-inch pieces, or baking chips

1/3 cup heavy whipping cream

6 tablespoons unsalted butter, cut into 1/4-inch pieces

1/2 cup sprinkles, red, green and white mixed together

1/2 cup walnuts, toasted and finely chopped

1/4 cup flavored good-quality cocoa powder

1/2 cup candy canes, chopped

76 mini cupcake liners

INSTRUCTIONS

1. In a small saucepan, bring the cream to just a simmer.

2. Add the butter and stir well until melted.

3. Place the chocolate in the cream mixture and stir until smooth.

4. Pour into a bowl and refrigerate the chocolate mixture until slightly firm, about one hour.

5. Using a 1-inch teaspoon measuring scoop, portion the truffle mixture and roll into balls using the palms of your hands.

6. Immediately roll each ball into your choice of sprinkles, nuts, chocolate or candy canes to coat.

7. Place truffles on a parchment-lined baking sheet and refrigerate for one hour or longer to set.

8. Remove from baking sheet and place each truffle in a mini cupcake liner.

tip / If chocolate balls become hard before rolling, reroll as you coat each one to ensure toppings will stick.

BROWNIE CHOCOLATE CHIP COOKIE DOUGH BARS

In this rich dessert, your favorite sweet treats unite in heavenly layers of brownie and chocolate chip cookie dough.

SERVES 9 | PREP 75 MINS | BAKE 9 MINS

INGREDIENTS

Brownies

1/4 teaspoon baking powder

1/3 cup cocoa powder

1/4 teaspoon salt

1/2 cup flour

1 tablespoon butter
(to grease pan)

1/2 cup vegetable oil

1 cup sugar

2 large eggs

1 teaspoon vanilla

Cookie dough batter

2-1/4 cups flour

1 teaspoon salt

2 sticks unsalted butter, softened

3/4 cup sugar

3/4 cup brown sugar

1 teaspoon vanilla extract

3 tablespoons milk

Chocolate ganache

2 cups chocolate morsels

2 cups dark chocolate,
finely chopped

1 cup heavy cream

Chocolate shavings (for garnish)

INSTRUCTIONS

Brownies

1. Preheat oven to 350F.

2. Place all dry ingredients for brownies (baking powder, cocoa powder, salt and flour) in large bowl and mix well.

3. Mix oil and sugar in bowl and mix until well-blended.

4. Add eggs and vanilla. Stir until blended.

5. Stir dry ingredients into the oil and sugar mixture.

6. Grease two 8x8-inch square pans with butter.

7. Pour batter evenly between greased pans.

8. Bake brownies for eight to nine minutes, or until sides just begin to pull away.

9. Cool completely in baking pan.

10. Tip: Slide knife around edges of brownies to loosen them so later removal is easier.

11. While brownies bake and cool, make no-bake cookie dough.

Cookie dough

1. In medium-sized bowl, mix flour and salt.

2. In separate mixing bowl, cream sugar, brown sugar and butter.

3. Add vanilla extract.

4. Slowly add flour mixture 1/2 cup at a time.

5. Once fully combined, add milk one tablespoon at a time, until cookie dough is loose enough to spread.

6. Fold in chocolate morsels and chill until ready to assemble.

Ganache

1. Heat cream in small saucepan until it just begins to boil.
2. Add chopped chocolate, stirring until completely melted and smooth.

To assemble

1. Remove brownie from one pan.
2. Add layer of cookie dough to brownies left in its pan: spread no-bake cookie dough over it until it covers brownie completely.
3. Layer second brownie over cookie dough. Spread another layer of cookie dough. There are now four layers in the pan
4. Pour ganache over the brownie-cookie dough layers
5. Place in refrigerator and allow to cool and set before serving.
6. Remove and garnish with chocolate shavings.
7. Cut into bars and serve.

PUMPKIN PECAN CHEESECAKE BARS

These deeply satisfying dessert bars deliver melt-in-your-mouth bites of spiced pumpkin filling on top of a brown sugar shortbread-style crust studded with pecans.

SERVES 12 | PREP 30 MINS | COOK 50 MINS

INGREDIENTS

1 cup all-purpose flour

1/3 cup brown sugar, packed

5 tablespoons cold unsalted butter, cut into cubes

1 cup pecans, finely chopped

1 (8-ounce) package cream cheese, softened

3/4 cup coconut sugar

1/2 cup canned pumpkin puree

2 eggs, whisked

1 teaspoon pure vanilla extract

1-1/2 teaspoons ground cinnamon

1 teaspoon ground pumpkin pie spice

INSTRUCTIONS

1. Preheat oven to 350F.

2. In a large bowl, mix together the flour and brown sugar.

3. Using a pastry cutter, blend in the butter until crumbly.

4. Stir in the pecans and set aside a 3/4-cup portion of the mixture for the topping.

5. Spray an 8-inch square baking dish with cooking spray. Press the remaining crumb mixture into the baking dish.

6. Bake for 15 minutes or until the edges are lightly browned.

7. Cool on a wire rack.

8. In a large bowl and using a handheld mixer, beat cream cheese and coconut sugar until smooth. Add the pumpkin puree, eggs, vanilla, cinnamon and pumpkin pie spice. Mix until well-blended.

9. Pour the pumpkin filling over the crust.

10. Sprinkle the top of the filling with the reserved crumb mixture.

11. Return the baking dish to the oven and bake for an additional 30 to 35 minutes or until the top is golden brown.

12. Cool on a wire rack, then cut into bars.

tip / Store these bars in the refrigerator.

SWEET POTATO CAKE WITH MARSHMALLOW FROSTING

Swap your traditional sweet potato casserole for this decadent sweet potato dessert.

SERVES 12 | PREP 50 MINS | COOK 60 MINS

INGREDIENTS

Cake batter

2-1/4 cups all-purpose flour

2 teaspoons baking powder

1 teaspoon baking soda

1/2 teaspoon salt

1 tablespoon ground cinnamon

1/2 teaspoon freshly grated nutmeg

1 teaspoon ground ginger

1/8 teaspoon ground cloves

1 cup unsalted butter, softened

1 cup granulated sugar

1/2 cup light brown sugar, packed

3 eggs

1 teaspoon pure vanilla extract

1-1/2 cups fresh sweet potato puree (about three medium sweet potatoes)

3/4 cup buttermilk

Pecan crisp

1/4 cup all-purpose flour

1/4 cup pecan pieces

1/4 cup rolled oats

1/2 cup light brown sugar, packed

3 tablespoons unsalted butter, softened

Marshmallow glaze

1 cup marshmallow creme

1/4 cup powdered sugar

3 to 4 teaspoons heavy whipping cream

INSTRUCTIONS

1. Preheat oven to 350F.

2. In a medium-sized bowl, whisk together flour, baking powder, baking soda, salt, cinnamon, nutmeg, ginger and cloves. Set aside.

3. In the bowl of a stand mixer fitted with the paddle attachment, combine butter, granulated sugar and brown sugar. Beat until the ingredients are well-blended, light and fluffy.

4. Beat in eggs one at a time.

5. Fold in the vanilla extract.

6. Incorporate dry ingredients into the wet ingredients a little at a time, alternating with the buttermilk.

7. Fold in the sweet potato puree, mix well.

8. Generously grease and flour a Bundt pan and spoon the batter into the pan.

9. Bake for 35 to 45 minutes or until a toothpick inserted in the center comes out clean.

10. Allow the cake to cool in the pan until the sides of the pan are warm to the touch.

11. Carefully remove cake from the pan and allow it to cool completely on a cooling rack.

12. In a medium-sized bowl, combine flour, pecans, oats, light brown sugar and softened butter. Mix well.

13. Line a baking sheet with foil. Spread the topping mixture onto the baking sheet in a single layer.

14. Bake for 10 to 15 minutes or until golden, tossing halfway through the cooking time.

15. Allow the pecan crisp topping to cool completely. It will become firmer as it cools. Set aside.

16. In a bowl, combine marshmallow cream, powdered sugar and milk. Using a handheld mixer, beat until well-blended. The mixture will be silky smooth and pourable.

17. When the cake has completely cooled, place it on a cake plate and pour the marshmallow frosting over the top and sides of the cake.

18. Sprinkle the top of the cake and around the bottom of the cake plate with the pecan crisp.

19. Refrigerate the cake to firm up the frosting.

PUMPKIN ROLL WITH CREAM CHEESE FILLING

Rich flavors of pumpkin, cinnamon and ginger are rolled up with a sweet and buttery cream cheese filling for a delightful seasonal treat.

SERVES 8-10 | PREP 35 MINS | COOK 15 MINS

INGREDIENTS

Cake

3/4 cup all-purpose flour, plus extra for dusting

1/2 teaspoon baking powder

1/2 teaspoon baking soda

1/2 teaspoon ground cinnamon

1/4 teaspoon ground cloves

1/4 teaspoon ground ginger

1/4 teaspoon salt

3 large eggs

1 cup granulated sugar

2/3 cup canned pumpkin (not pumpkin pie filling)

1/4 cup powdered sugar (to sprinkle on the towel)

Filling

1 (8-ounce) package cream cheese, softened to room temperature

1 cup powdered sugar, sifted

6 tablespoons unsalted butter, at room temperature

1 teaspoon pure vanilla extract

Powdered sugar, to garnish

INSTRUCTIONS

Cake

1. Preheat oven to 375F.

2. Spray a 15x10-inch baking sheet with cooking spray. Line with a fitted piece of parchment paper and spray the pan and parchment. Generously dust the baking sheet with flour and tap out the excess.

3. In a medium-sized mixing bowl, combine flour, baking powder, baking soda, cinnamon, cloves, ginger and salt.

4. In the bowl of a stand mixer fitted with the paddle attachment, combine the eggs and granulated sugar and beat on medium until thick. Pour in the pumpkin puree and beat on medium until combined.

5. Add the flour mixture and continue to beat on low until well-combined.

6. Using a spatula, spread the pumpkin mixture evenly onto the prepared baking sheet.

7. Bake for 13 to 15 minutes or until the top of the cake springs back when gently pressed with a finger.

Filling

While the cake is baking, make the cream cheese filling. In a large mixing bowl combine the cream cheese, remaining powdered sugar, butter and vanilla. Use an electric handheld mixer to beat the ingredients until creamy and smooth.

Assembly

1. Spread a thin kitchen towel out flat on a clean surface. Sprinkle the towel with the powdered sugar.

2. Immediately loosen the cake from the baking sheet and turn it out onto the prepared kitchen towel.

3. Carefully peel the paper from the cake. Gently roll up the cake and towel together, starting with narrow end. Cool the cake on a wire rack.

4. Carefully unroll cake, keeping the towel underneath the cake. Evenly spread the cream cheese filling over the cake all the way to the edges. Gently reroll the cake, taking care to not press the filling out of the ends. Wrap the cake in plastic wrap and refrigerate for at least one hour.

5. Sprinkle the cake with additional powdered sugar before serving, if desired.

6. Slice crosswise and serve.

Drinks & cocktails

RICH MOCHA EGGNOG

This eggnog adds a new twist to the old favorite with the addition of rich, creamy chocolate.

MAKES 2 QUARTS | PREP 20 MINS

INGREDIENTS

1 cup high-quality chocolate, chopped into 1/4" pieces

1 tablespoon unsweetened, high-quality cocoa powder

3 cups milk

2 cups heavy cream

8 eggs (separated)

2/3 cup sugar

2 cups bourbon

Shaved chocolate and freshly-grated nutmeg to garnish

INSTRUCTIONS

1. In a large bowl, mix together the chocolate and cocoa powder.

2. In a small saucepan, bring 2 cups of milk to a simmer over medium heat.

3. Pour warm milk over chocolate and whisk well until chocolate is melted. Add remaining milk and cream, then set aside.

4. In the large mixing bowl of a stand mixer, place egg whites. Then whisk on low until frothy, about 30 seconds.

5. Increase the speed to medium and beat until the egg whites are thick and frothy, about 90 seconds.

6. With mixer running, slowly stream in half the sugar and beat until incorporated, about 30 seconds. Place the beaten egg whites in a large bowl and reserve.

7. Place the bowl back on the stand mixer. Add egg yolks and remaining sugar. Whisk at medium speed until yolks are thickened and pale yellow, about 1 minute. Set speed to low and slowly add milk/chocolate mixture and whisk until fully incorporated, about 1 minute.

8. Add bourbon and mix until combined.

9. Using a spatula, gently fold egg whites into chocolate mixture.

10. Pour into glasses and serve garnished with shaved chocolate and grated nutmeg.

ORANGECELLO AND HONEY MARTINI

SERVES 1 | PREP 38 MINS (INCLUDES STEEPING TIME FOR SIMPLE SYRUP)

INGREDIENTS

1 cup water

1 cup honey

10 sprigs of thyme

2 ounces vodka

2 ounces orangecello

1/4 cup orange juice

1 tablespoon honey thyme simple syrup

Sprig of thyme as garnish

Honey

Small plate of white sugar

INSTRUCTIONS

1. In a small saucepan, whisk together water and honey. Bring to a boil.

2. Pour the warm simple syrup into a glass bowl and add the sprigs of thyme. Allow it to steep for 30 minutes and cool completely before using in the martini.

3. Rim a glass dipped in honey. Roll in white sugar. Set aside.

4. Add ice to a martini shaker.

5. Pour the vodka, orangecello, orange juice and 1 tablespoon simple syrup together into the shaker.

6. Shake until cold.

7. Strain into a martini glass.

8. Garnish with a sprig of thyme.

TOASTED HOT CHOCOLATE

SERVES 4 | PREP 5 MINS

INGREDIENTS

Prepared hot chocolate

4 ounces coffee liqueur

2 ounces amaretto liqueur

2 ounces Bailey's Irish Cream

4 marshmallows, lightly toasted

Whipped cream

Crushed peppermint candy canes

INSTRUCTIONS

1. Combine coffee liqueur, amaretto liqueur and Bailey's Irish Cream. Stir.

2. Divide alcohol mixture evenly among 4 mugs.

3. Fill each mug with hot cocoa and stir to blend all ingredients.

4. Top with whipped cream.

5. Place a toasted marshmallow atop each mug of hot cocoa.

6. Sprinkle with crushed peppermint just before serving.

tip / Toast your marshmallows indoors by broiling them for a few seconds on a cookie sheet inside the oven!

SIMPLE MAPLE BACON EGGNOG

SERVES 1 | PREP 4 MINS

INGREDIENTS

6 ounces store-bought nonalcoholic eggnog

2 ounces bourbon

1/2 ounce maple syrup

1 bacon strip

Pinch of nutmeg

INSTRUCTIONS

1. Stir maple syrup and bourbon together.

2. Add chilled eggnog.

3. Garnish with bacon strip and a pinch of nutmeg.

tip / A splash of bourbon adds a little kick to this unique drink.

PEPPERMINT WHITE RUSSIAN COCKTAIL

MAKES 2 DRINKS | PREP 20 MINS

INGREDIENTS

Peppermint candy simple syrup:

Crushed peppermint candies

1/4 cup sugar

1 cup water

Cocktail:

4 ounces vodka

3-1/2 ounces coffee liqueur (recommended: Kahlua)

Splash half-and-half

INSTRUCTIONS

Peppermint candy simple syrup:

1. Combine candies, sugar and water.

2. Simmer, stirring often, until melted.

3. Cool in refrigerator.

Cocktail:

1. Combine vodka, coffee liqueur and splash of half-and-half in a glass with ice.

2. Add 1 tablespoon simple syrup.

3. Stir well.

CHOCOLATE ESPRESSO MARTINI

SERVES 2 | PREP 18 MINS (INCLUDING 10 MINUTES CHILLING TIME)

INGREDIENTS

2 ounces good-quality semisweet chocolate, finely chopped

1/3 cup brewed espresso, chilled

1/3 cup Kahlua

1/3 cup vanilla-flavored vodka

1/4 cup water

Ice

2 large strawberries

INSTRUCTIONS

1. In small bowl, combine chocolate and 1/4 cup water. Stir well.

2. Place bowl over pan of barely simmering water. Stir until chocolate is completely melted and mixture is smooth, about 2 minutes. Set aside to cool.

3. Dip rims of 2 martini glasses into melted chocolate, allowing excess chocolate to drip back into bowl.

4. Chill glasses in freezer for 10 minutes.

5. In pitcher, mix espresso, Kahlua and vodka.

6. Fill cocktail shaker with ice.

7. Add Kahlua mixture and shake for 10 seconds.

8. Garnish with strawberry on each glass.

9. Strain mixture into prepared glasses and serve.

JALAPEÑO CRANBERRY COSMOS

SERVES 1 | PREP 3 MINS

INGREDIENTS

1 ounce vodka

1 ounce lime juice

1 ounce reserved jalapeño cranberry sauce juice (recipe on page 172)

INSTRUCTIONS

1. Fill a cocktail shaker with ice

2. Add the vodka and lime, strain into a martini glass.

3. Add the reserved cranberry sauce and stir. Serve.

AMARETTO CRANBERRY KISS

SERVES 4 | PREP 6 MINS

INGREDIENTS

16 ounces cranberry juice cocktail

8 ounces vodka

4 ounces amaretto

3 ounces fresh orange juice

Clementines, peeled and separated into segments, for garnish

Rosemary sprig, for garnish

Ice

INSTRUCTIONS

1. Mix cranberry juice, vodka, amaretto and orange juice into a pitcher.

2. Cover with plastic wrap and chill until ready to serve.

3. Fill cocktail shaker with ice cubes.

4. Pour eight ounces of cranberry juice cocktail mixture into a shaker.

5. Cover with lid and shake vigorously.

6. Strain into martini glasses.

7. Garnish each glass with a clementine segment and sprig of fresh rosemary.

tip / Amaretto is a sweet Italian liqueur with a distinct almond flavor.

POMEGRANATE THYME BUBBLY ROSÉ

SERVES 1 | PREP 3 MINS

INGREDIENTS

1/2 cup pomegranate juice

3 tablespoons simple syrup

Sparkling rosé wine

1 sprig of thyme

INSTRUCTIONS

1. Combine juice, sugar, water and simple syrup.

2. Pour into flute and top with rosé.

3. Garnish with thyme.

VEGAN SPICED-APPLE MARGARITA

Made with a tasty blend of apple and lime juices, reposado tequila, agave and a dash of cinnamon, each sip is an autumn party in your mouth.

SERVES 1 | PREP 8 MINUTES, PLUS ADDITIONAL CHILLING TIME FOR SIMPLE SYRUP

INGREDIENTS

Agave nectar simple syrup

1/4 cup agave nectar

1/4 cup water

Rim blend

1 teaspoon coconut sugar

1 teaspoon sea salt

1/2 teaspoon ground Vietnamese cinnamon

Lime wedge

Margarita

2 ounces reposado tequila

1-1/2 to 2 ounces apple juice or apple cider

3/4 ounce fresh lime juice

3/4 teaspoon agave simple syrup (see recipe below)

Dash ground cinnamon

Garnish

1 star of anise

Thin slice of apple

INSTRUCTIONS

Agave simple syrup

1. In a small saucepan over medium heat, combine the water and agave nectar.

2. Warm, stirring frequently, just until the water and agave are completely combined.

3. Remove the saucepan from heat and set it aside to cool.

Rim blend

1. On a small plate, use a fork to blend the sugar, salt and cinnamon together.

2. Run a wedge of lime around the top of a glass, then turn the glass down at a 45-degree angle and roll the top of the glass through the sugar, salt and cinnamon blend to coat the rim.

3. Fill the glass with ice and set aside.

Margarita

1. Fill a cocktail shaker with ice.

2. Pour in tequila, apple juice or cider, lime juice, agave simple syrup and cinnamon.

3. Put the lid on the shaker and shake the cocktail vigorously for about 20 seconds.

4. Strain the cocktail into the prepared glass.

5. Garnish with a star of anise and a fresh apple slice.

HOLIDAY-SPICED SANGRIA

With apple cider, brandy, orange and lemon juices and a spiced simple syrup, this is a seasonal take on the classic.

SERVES 6 | PREP 12 MINUTES, PLUS 2-4 HOURS TO CHILL

INGREDIENTS

Spiced simple syrup

2 cups water

1 cup sugar

Black peppercorn

Cinnamon sticks

Star anise and clove
(to preference)

1/4 cup sliced ginger root

Cocktail

1 bottle dry red wine (we used Spanish tempranillo)

1 cup apple cider

4 ounces (1/2 cup) brandy

1/4 cup orange juice

2 ounces lemon juice

1/2 cup spiced simple syrup

INSTRUCTIONS

1. To prepare spiced simple syrup, combine all syrup ingredients and stir until sugar is dissolved. (Store any extra in refrigerator.)

2. Combine all cocktail ingredients and mix well.

3. Chill for 2 to 4 hours.

4. Before serving, garnish with fruit (suggestions: oranges, apples, pears).

5. Store in refrigerator for up to 2 days.

Recipe by Sally McKenney

APPLE CIDER SANGRIA

This irresistible white wine sangria is filled with fall's best flavors like apple, cider, citrus, cinnamon and pear.

SERVES 6-8 | PREP 30 MIN PLUS CHILLING

(DF) (EF) (GF) (GR) (NF) (Q) (VG)

INGREDIENTS

2 cinnamon sticks, plus
more for serving

2 medium apples, thinly sliced

1 medium pear, thinly sliced

1 medium orange, thinly sliced

2/3 cup pomegranate seeds

1 bottle white wine
like Pinot Grigio

2 cups apple cider

1/2 cup brandy

1/4 cup orange juice

2 tablespoons lemon juice

Club soda, for serving

INSTRUCTIONS

1. Place the cinnamon sticks and fruit into a large pitcher. Add wine, apple cider, brandy, orange juice, and lemon juice. Allow to sit in the refrigerator for 3 to 24 hours (6 to 8 hours is best).

2. Pour the sangria and fruit into glasses. Add a splash of club soda. Garnish with a cinnamon stick, if desired.

HOLIDAY ORANGE WASSAIL PUNCH

Wassail is a spicy, sweet, hot mulled cider that used to be made with beer or mead, apples and seasonings.

MAKES 6 QUARTS | PREP 15 MINS

DF EF GF GR NF VG

INGREDIENTS

1 bottle (64 ounces) orange juice

1 bottle (32 ounces) cranberry juice cocktail

1 12-ounce can frozen lemonade concentrate, thawed and undiluted

6 ounces apple cider

1 tablespoon vanilla extract

1 stick cinnamon

1 tablespoon ground cloves

2 oranges, sliced

INSTRUCTIONS

1. Combine orange juice, cranberry juice cocktail, lemonade and apple cider in a large stockpot.

2. Mix in vanilla extract, cinnamon, cloves and orange slices.

3. Cook uncovered over medium heat until heated through.

4. Serve warm in mugs.

tip / To make an adult version, add 3 cups bourbon.

SWEET AND FRUITY FAUX CHAMPAGNE

Sweet and bubbly, this a fun toasting mocktail for kids. It's also great for adults who don't indulge in alcohol but still want to enjoy something festive.

SERVES 1 | PREP 2 MINS

INGREDIENTS

2 ounces white grape juice

1 ounce orange juice

Ginger ale

Frozen white grapes

INSTRUCTIONS

1. Pour white grape juice into champagne flute.

2. Pour orange juice on top of grape juice.

3. Top with ginger ale and stir.

4. Garnish with a speared frozen grape and add a festive straw.

tip / If you want to save a few calories, try using diet ginger ale and your favorite sugar-free drink mix or flavored sparkling water.

BOOZY PUMPKIN WHITE HOT CHOCOLATE

Gourmet hot chocolate with a kick couldn't be easier. All you need is a handful of key ingredients, a saucepan and a few minutes.

SERVES 2-4 | PREP 10 MINS

INGREDIENTS

1/2 cup chopped white chocolate

2-1/2 cups whole milk, divided

1/4 cup pumpkin puree

1/4 teaspoon pumpkin pie spice plus extra for garnish

1 ounce Kahlua coffee liqueur

Whipped cream

Caramel sauce

INSTRUCTIONS

1. In a saucepan over low-medium heat, combine white chocolate and 1/2 cup of the milk. Cook, continuously whisking, for 3 to 4 minutes or until the white chocolate is melted and the mixture is smooth.

2. Add the remainder of the milk, pumpkin puree and pumpkin pie spice, whisking the ingredients until well-combined. Continue to heat, whisking often, until the mixture is hot.

3. Pour a small amount of the hot chocolate into 2 to 4 serving glasses and add 1 ounce of Kahlua to each glass. Stir to combine.

4. Top each glass with the rest of the white hot chocolate and stir.

5. Garnish with whipped cream, caramel sauce and a dash of pumpkin pie spice.

tip / Be sure to stir continuously while cooking because it can scald quickly.

PUMPKIN FIZZ COCKTAIL

Pumpkin, honey, citrus, ginger and bourbon combine in this fizzy drink that will suit everyone's style.

SERVES 1 | PREP 6 MINS

INGREDIENTS

Honey and brown sugar
for glass rim

1 ounce pumpkin puree

1 teaspoon honey

1/2 whole lemon, juice only

1 1/2 ounces bourbon

1/2 bottle ginger beer

1 long slice of lemon, twisted

INSTRUCTIONS

1. Pour a bit of honey into a small plate. Sprinkle brown sugar onto a second small plate.

2. Slide the rim of a highball glass in the honey to make it sticky, then rim the edge of the glass with brown sugar. Set aside.

3. Place pumpkin puree, honey and juice from the half lemon in a cocktail shaker.

4. Muddle the mixture.

5. Add ice and bourbon to the shaker. Shake vigorously for 10 to 15 seconds.

6. Use tongs to place additional ice into the highball glass, being careful with the brown sugar rim.

7. Strain the contents of the shaker into the prepared highball glass.

8. Top with ginger beer and stir gently.

9. Garnish the cocktail with a lemon twist and serve immediately.

DULCE DE LECHE HOT CHOCOLATE

Move over powdered hot cocoa, dulce de leche hot chocolate is the real deal. Thick, sweet and savory all at the same time, it will warm you up from the inside out.

SERVES 4 | PREP 15 MINS

INGREDIENTS

1 (14-ounce) can dulce de leche sweetened condensed milk

1/3 cup unsweetened cocoa powder

1 teaspoon ground cinnamon

Dash of ground nutmeg

3 cups whole milk

1 tablespoon chocolate chips

1 teaspoon pure vanilla extract

Kosher salt

Sprinkle of ancho chili powder for each cup

Whipped cream

Chocolate shavings for garnish

INSTRUCTIONS

1. In a large saucepan over medium-high heat, combine the sweetened condensed milk, cocoa powder, cinnamon, milk, vanilla and a small pinch of salt.

2. Stir continuously until small bubbles appear but do not allow the mixture to come to a boil.

3. Lower the heat to medium and stir in the chocolate chips and ancho chili powder. Whisk well until the chocolate has melted. Simmer until ready to serve.

4. Pour the hot chocolate into mugs, top with whipped cream and garnish with chocolate shavings.

5. Serve immediately.

tip / If serving kids, feel free to skip the ancho chili powder. And for the adults, add a splash of Bailey's Irish Cream.

HOT APPLE CIDER
WITH BUTTERED RUM

Quick and easy to prepare, this butter rum is smooth, fruity, warm and a little boozy. Perfect for sipping after your holiday feast.

SERVES 3 | PREP 20 MINS

INGREDIENTS

1 (24.5-ounce) bottle apple cider

2 tablespoons butter

1/2 large apple, cored and sliced, plus more thinly sliced for garnish

1/2 large pear, cored and sliced, plus more thinly sliced for garnish

1 thumb-sized ginger piece, peeled, thinly sliced

1 whole cinnamon stick

1/4 teaspoon ground allspice

Pinch ground cloves

1/4 cup packed brown sugar

1/2 cup Myers's dark rum

Extra long cinnamon sticks for garnish

INSTRUCTIONS

1. Place apple cider, butter, apple and pear slices, ginger, cinnamon stick, allspice, cloves and brown sugar in a large saucepan. Bring to a boil over high heat.

2. Reduce the heat and simmer for 10 minutes, whisking occasionally.

3. Remove the pan from the heat and stir in the dark rum. Whisk until well-blended.

4. Strain the mixture, discarding the fruit pieces and spices.

5. Pour the apple cider into large serving mugs.

6. Garnish each mug with a thinly sliced apple and pear and a cinnamon stick.

7. Serve immediately.

tip / Use a mandoline to get perfectly sliced fruit for a touch of extra class.

Leftovers

LEFTOVER TURKEY SHEPHERD'S PIE

Once you dig your fork into cheesy layers of mashed potatoes, juicy shredded turkey and vegetables, you'll want to roast a bigger bird next year for the leftovers.

SERVES 4–6 | PREP 15 MINS | COOK 45 MINS

INGREDIENTS

2 tablespoons butter

1 onion, diced

1 green bell pepper, diced

3 cloves garlic, minced

2 cups shredded turkey meat

1 can (14-1/2 ounces or 1-1/2 cups) crushed tomatoes

1 teaspoon hot sauce

Salt and pepper, to taste

1-1/2 tablespoons Italian seasoning

3 tablespoons fresh basil, cut in chiffonade

Salt and freshly ground black pepper to taste

2 cups mashed potatoes

3/4 cup shredded mozzarella cheese

1/4 cup shredded Parmesan cheese

Fresh parsley

INSTRUCTIONS

1. Preheat oven to 375F. Place baking dish on parchment-lined baking tray.

2. In large skillet over medium-high heat, melt butter. Add onion, green bell pepper and garlic. Cook, stirring often, until onion is tender and translucent.

3. Add shredded turkey, crushed tomatoes and hot sauce. Season with salt and pepper. Cook, stirring occasionally, for 5 minutes. Stir in Italian seasoning and fresh basil.

4. Pour turkey mixture into baking dish. Cover mixture with mashed potatoes, using spatula to completely cover turkey mixture.

5. Evenly sprinkle shredded mozzarella and Parmesan cheeses over mashed potatoes.

6. Bake for 30 minutes or until cheese is melted and bubbly.

7. Garnish with fresh parsley. Serve hot.

TURKEY "CARNITAS" TACOS

Add some fresh seasonings like oranges, onions and bay leaves, and toppings like pico de gallo, for a fresh take on leftover turkey.

SERVING AMOUNT VARIES | PREP 20 MINS | COOK 1 HR 10 MINS

INGREDIENTS

Any amount leftover cooked dark-meat turkey

1 orange per pound of leftover turkey meat, preferably sour

1 medium onion per pound of leftover turkey meat

2 bay leaves per pound of leftover turkey meat

2 tablespoons vegetable oil or turkey fat per pound of leftover turkey meat

Kosher salt

1/2 red onion, diced

4 ounces pico de gallo

2 limes, cut in wedges

12 corn or wheat tortillas

Cilantro sprigs

INSTRUCTIONS

1. Combine turkey (including bones), orange, onion and bay leaf in stock pot. Mixture should fit snugly. Add enough water to cover halfway up sides of pot.

2. Cover and bring to boil, then reduce to simmer and cook until turkey is fall-off-the-bone tender, about 1 hour.

3. Drain stock and save for another use.

4. Discard orange, onion, bones and bay leaves. Place turkey in another bowl.

5. Shred turkey with a couple of forks.

6. Heat oil or fat in cast-iron skillet over medium-high heat until it begins to shimmer.

7. Working in batches, add turkey and spread into even layer. Cook, without stirring, until meat is well-browned and crisp on bottom, about 5 minutes. Stir turkey to incorporate crisp bits and introduce new soft bits to bottom. Continue until turkey is as crisp as desired. Season with salt.

8. Assemble carnitas by warming tortillas, then adding: crisp turkey, red onion and pico de gallo. Squeeze fresh lime juice over carnitas and garnish with cilantro.

tip / When cooled, pour the remaining stock into quart-sized reclosable bags for easy use in other recipes.

LEFTOVER TURKEY TAQUITOS WITH NUTTY BUFFALO DIPPING SAUCE

Taquitos are deep-fried tortillas stuffed with seasoned meat—in this case, turkey.

MAKES 18–24 | PREP 20 MINS | COOK 25 MINS

INGREDIENTS

Buffalo dipping sauce

1 cup raw unsalted pistachios, coarsely chopped

1/3 cup Buffalo hot sauce

1/4 to 1/2 cup water, if needed

Taquitos

2 cups leftover turkey, shredded or cubed

3 tablespoons butter, divided

1/2 yellow onion, diced

2 stalks celery, diced

1 teaspoon salt

1 teaspoon ground cumin

4 ounces cream cheese, room temperature

5 ounces blue cheese, room temperature

2 tablespoons butter

2-1/2 tablespoons Buffalo hot sauce

2 cups vegetable oil

18 to 24 white or yellow corn-wheat tortillas

Additional hot sauce

INSTRUCTIONS

Buffalo dipping sauce

1. In small bowl, combine pistachios and Buffalo sauce until well blended.

2. Drizzle in water and mix to desired consistency.

3. Set aside to serve as dipping sauce.

Taquitos

1. Place shredded turkey in medium bowl. Set aside.

2. In large skillet on medium heat, melt 1 tablespoon butter. Add onions, celery, salt and cumin, and sauté for 3 to 5 minutes, or until onions are translucent.

3. Add cream cheese, blue cheese, additional 2 tablespoons butter and Buffalo sauce into large skillet. Stirring frequently, allow to simmer over medium heat until cheese has melted.

4. Place shredded turkey into skillet of cheese mixture. Stir until well combined, then remove from heat. Set aside.

5. Pour oil into deep skillet. Heat oil until reaches 350F.

6. Fry one tortilla at a time for 6 to 10 seconds; turn over and fry for 4 seconds more.

7. Remove and drain on paper towel. Repeat process until all are lightly fried. Note: This step helps tortilla roll better and keeps it from cracking.

8. On chopping board or dinner plate, lay one corn tortilla out flat. Arrange 1-1/2 tablespoons

shredded turkey mixture in center of tortilla. Roll up tortilla tightly until it resembles cigar. Secure ends with toothpick.

9. Deep-fry taquitos two at a time until brown and crispy.

10. Remove from oil and place on paper towels to drain. Blot with paper towels to remove excess grease.

11. When cool enough to touch, remove toothpicks.

12. Serve immediately with Buffalo dipping sauce.

LEFTOVER TURKEY ENCHILADAS

Generously stuffed turkey and cheese enchiladas are snugly arranged in a casserole dish, then topped with corn, black beans and more cheese.

SERVES 22–24 | PREP 25 MINS | COOK 1 HR 20 MINS

INGREDIENTS

3 tablespoons plus 1/2 cup vegetable oil, divided

1 small red onion, diced

2 leeks, green part removed, white part sliced thinly

4 cloves garlic, minced

2 tablespoons ground cumin

5 cups leftover cooked turkey (dark and white meat), shredded

3 plum tomatoes, diced

4 (15-ounce) cans red enchilada sauce, divided

2-1/2 tablespoons chipotle chiles in adobo, diced

1/4 cup fresh cilantro, roughly chopped

24 thick corn tortillas

3 ears corn, cooked, kernels cut from ear

1 (15-ounce) can black beans, rinsed, drained

4 cups shredded Mexican cheese, for filling and topping

INSTRUCTIONS

1. Preheat oven to 350F.

2. Heat 3 tablespoons oil in large skillet over medium heat.

3. Add onions and leeks. Cook, stirring often, for 6 to 8 minutes or until onions and leeks are transparent.

4. Add garlic and cumin. Cook, stirring often, for 2 more minutes.

5. Add shredded turkey, diced tomatoes, 2 cans enchilada sauce, chipotle chiles, and cilantro. Reduce heat to low and simmer for 30 minutes.

6. In a small skillet over medium heat, heat remaining 1/2 cup oil.

7. Working with one tortilla at a time, submerge tortilla in hot oil and allow to soften for 10 seconds; turn and heat for another 5 seconds. Set tortilla on stack of paper towels to drain.

8. Repeat process until all tortillas are cooked.

9. Spread 1/2 can red enchilada sauce in bottom of large casserole dish. Set aside.

10. Place tortilla on plate. Add enough turkey mixture, about 1/4 cup, to line center of tortilla. Sprinkle turkey filling with shredded cheese. Roll tortilla around turkey filling and place it seam-side down in casserole dish. Repeat until all tortillas are filled or all filling is gone.

11. Pour remaining 1-1/2 cans enchilada sauce over top of turkey-filled tortilla casserole. Add any leftover turkey mixture to tops of enchiladas.

12. Sprinkle corn kernels, black beans and remaining shredded cheese over top of enchiladas.

13. Bake uncovered in oven for 30 minutes or until sauce is bubbling and cheese is melted.
14. Remove casserole dish from oven and allow enchiladas to cool for 5 minutes.
15. Serve hot.

HOLIDAY LEFTOVERS POPPERS

Each bite has a panko-breaded crunch that gives way to a comfort-food layer of mashed potatoes wrapped around a tasty center of stuffing, turkey and Gruyère cheese.

SERVES 6 | PREP 1 HR, INCLUDING 30 MINS SETTING TIME | COOK 20-25 MINS

INGREDIENTS

2 cups stuffing, broken into small-sized pieces

1 cup leftover turkey, finely chopped

3/4 cup shredded Gruyère cheese

3 tablespoons minced fresh parsley, plus extra for garnish

4 to 5 cups cold mashed potatoes

1 cup all-purpose flour

1 large egg, whisked

2 cups panko bread crumbs

2 cups peanut oil

1-1/2 cups hot turkey gravy for dipping

INSTRUCTIONS

1. In large bowl, combine stuffing, turkey, cheese and parsley. Mix until well-blended.

2. Line two baking sheets with parchment paper.

3. Form balls of stuffing mixture using 2-tablespoon measuring spoon. Roll all mixture into balls and place on parchment-lined baking sheet.

4. Transfer baking sheet to freezer and allow leftovers bites to set for 30 minutes.

5. Fill deep cast-iron casserole pot with enough oil to submerge balls. Heat oil to 365F and keep at constant temperature.

6. Set up assembly line of ingredients to finish making balls. Fill first bowl with mashed potatoes, second bowl with flour, third bowl with whisked egg and fourth bowl with panko bread crumbs.

7. Remove balls from freezer and wrap about 4 tablespoons cold mashed potatoes around each ball.

8. Next, gently roll each ball in flour and then transfer to egg bowl. Using one hand, roll ball around to cover in egg. With your other hand, dip and cover ball in panko bread crumbs. Place prepared turkey balls on second parchment-lined baking sheet and continue forming until all ingredients are used.

9. Line baking sheet with paper towels. Working in batches, gently drop 2 to 3 balls into hot oil and fry until balls are golden brown, about 3 to 4 minutes. Remove balls with heatproof slotted spoon or spider skimmer and transfer to lined baking sheet to drain. Continue deep-frying remaining balls. Be sure to adjust heat as needed to keep oil at consistent 365F.

10. Garnish these bites of holiday leftovers with extra minced parsley.

11. Serve immediately with hot gravy for dipping.

LEFTOVER TURKEY CHILI-SMOTHERED SWEET POTATOES

With just a few ingredients from your pantry, you can make a tasty black bean and turkey chili that begs to be served in a hot and steamy sweet potato.

SERVES 4 | PREP 30 MINS | COOK 1 HR

INGREDIENTS

Sweet potatoes

2 tablespoons olive oil

4 sweet potatoes (8 to 12 ounces each)

Turkey chili

1 tablespoon olive oil

1 yellow onion, diced

2 cloves garlic, minced

1-1/2 cups leftover turkey, shredded or chopped

1 can black beans (15 ounces), rinsed and drained

1 can (8 ounces) tomato sauce

1 tablespoon tomato paste

1 tablespoon chili powder

1/2 teaspoon dried oregano

1/2 teaspoon ground cumin

1/2 cup water

Salt to taste

Topping

1/2 cup shredded cheddar cheese

Chopped fresh cilantro or green onions for garnish

INSTRUCTIONS

1. Preheat oven to 400F and line baking sheet with parchment paper.

2. Using up to 2 tablespoons olive oil, rub outside skins of each sweet potato. Prick a few times with fork.

3. Place sweet potatoes on baking sheet. Roast for 30 minutes, then turn and continue roasting for 1 hour or until very soft.

4. In large skillet over medium-high heat, add 1 tablespoon olive oil and heat for 1 minute.

5. Add onion and garlic, and saute for 3 to 4 minutes or until onions turn soft and transparent.

6. Stir in leftover turkey and cook for 2 minutes.

7. Add black beans, tomato sauce, tomato paste, chili powder, oregano, cumin and water. Stir to combine.

8. Bring chili to simmer, reduce heat to medium-low and simmer for 15 minutes. Taste and add salt, if needed.

9. Once sweet potatoes are finished baking, carefully slice each lengthwise to open but not cut through all way. Use fork to lightly mash insides.

10. Scoop about 3/4 cup chili over each sweet potato, then top with 2 tablespoons shredded cheese.

11. Return potatoes to oven for a few minutes to melt cheese.

12. Garnish with cilantro and sliced green onions just before serving.

LEFTOVER TURKEY POT PIE SOUP

This scrumptious recipe uses a garlicky cauliflower puree that becomes the luscious base for the soup.

SERVES 8 | PREP 30 MINS | COOK 40 MINS

INGREDIENTS

1-1/2 tablespoons olive oil

1 cup chopped yellow onion

1 cup diced carrot

1 cup diced celery

1 cup corn

1 cup sliced brown mushrooms

7 cups hot chicken broth, divided

2 cups diced, peeled russet potatoes

1 teaspoon fresh thyme

1 teaspoon chopped fresh rosemary

1 bay leaf, dried

3 cups leftover turkey, cubed or shredded

1 cup frozen peas

2 tablespoons butter

8 cloves garlic, minced

7 cups cauliflower florets, leave a few larger pieces

2-1/2 teaspoons kosher salt, more to taste

1 teaspoon freshly ground black pepper, more to taste

1/4 cup minced fresh parsley for garnish

INSTRUCTIONS

1. In a large, heavy-bottomed pot, heat olive oil over medium-high heat.

2. Add onion, carrot, celery, corn and mushrooms. Saute for 3 minutes.

3. Add 3 cups chicken broth along with potatoes, thyme, rosemary and bay leaf, stirring to combine.

4. Bring soup to a boil over high heat, then reduce heat to medium, cover with lid, and cook, stirring occasionally, for 15 to 20 minutes or until the potatoes are tender.

5. Reduce the heat to low and stir in the turkey and peas.

6. In a nonstick skillet over low heat, melt the butter. Add the garlic and cook, stirring often, for 5 to 6 minutes. Do not let the garlic brown. Remove from heat and set aside.

7. In a large pot over high heat, bring water to a boil. Add the cauliflower and cook, covered, for 7 to 10 minutes or until the cauliflower is fork-tender. Do not drain.

8. Using a slotted spoon, transfer the cauliflower pieces to a blender.

9. Add 2 cups of hot chicken broth and the garlic/butter mixture to the cauliflower. Blend for several minutes until the puree is smooth.

10. Stir the cauliflower puree into the turkey and vegetable mixture. Add more of the chicken broth to the soup to achieve desired consistency.

11. Add salt and black pepper to season. Remove the bay leaf.

12. Serve the soup hot, garnished with minced parsley.

CREAMY LEFTOVER TURKEY AND TORTELLINI SOUP

This fabulously creamy leftover turkey and tortellini soup is so thick, it comes close to being a stew.

SERVES 4 | PREP 20 MINS | COOK 20 MINS

INGREDIENTS

3 tablespoons butter

1/4 cup white onion, diced

1 celery stalk, diced

1/3 cup carrot, diced

1 clove garlic, diced

3 tablespoons flour

1/2 teaspoon salt

1/4 teaspoon fresh ground black pepper

1/2 teaspoon dried mustard

1/4 teaspoon dried sage

1/4 teaspoon dried thyme

2 cups milk

2 cups chicken or vegetable broth

1 pound cooked turkey, cubed into bite-sized pieces or shredded

1/3 cup frozen peas

9 ounces fresh, refrigerated cheese tortellini

INSTRUCTIONS

1. Melt butter in Dutch oven or large pot over medium heat. When melted, add onion, celery and carrot.

2. Cook, stirring occasionally, for about 5 minutes or until vegetables begin to soften. Add garlic and cook for about 30 seconds.

3. Add flour to mixture, and whisk to combine. It will be slightly clumpy. Add salt, black pepper, mustard, sage and thyme; mix.

4. Whisk in milk and broth, a little at a time. Whisk until smooth.

5. Bring mixture to boil, then reduce heat. Add turkey, peas and tortellini to mixture. Simmer for about 8 minutes.

6. The soup is very thick, so add more milk if desired.

tip / This recipe serves four, but you can easily double the ingredients to feed a crowd.

LEFTOVERS PASTRY POCKETS

Have some fun with these pockets that even the kids will love. Since all the ingredients are leftovers, and therefore fully cooked, all you have to do is bake the dough.

SERVES 3 | PREP 15 MINS | COOK 15-20 MINS .

INGREDIENTS

One 9-inch prepared pie dough

1/2 cup turkey, chopped

1/4 cup leftover gravy

2 tablespoons leftover cranberry sauce

1/3 cup leftover stuffing (optional)

1 egg

INSTRUCTIONS

1. Preheat oven to 400F.

2. Thaw pie dough until soft enough to handle. Trim edges to create large rectangle and cut four 4-by-8-inch rectangles.

3. Mix turkey and gravy. Scoop small portion into center of two rectangles. Place other desired fillings, such as cranberry sauce and stuffing, on top of turkey.

4. Carefully place other two rectangle dough pieces on top. Press fork around edges to close seams of pockets.

5. Place pockets on parchment-lined baking sheet. Whisk egg with 1 tablespoon water, and brush to create egg wash. Brush over top of pockets and cut slits on top of each. Bake for 15 to 20 minutes or until golden brown.

6. Let cool slightly. Serve warm.

LEFTOVER TURKEY PINWHEEL SANDWICHES

MAKES 24 PINWHEELS | PREP 18 MINS

INGREDIENTS

1 cup leftover cooked turkey, shredded or chopped

1/3 cup mayonnaise, or as desired

1 tablespoon carrots, finely chopped

1 tablespoon walnuts, finely chopped

1/2 tablespoon celery, finely chopped

1/2 teaspoon lemon zest

Salt and pepper

1 cup arugula

4 big slices sandwich bread, crusts and sides removed

INSTRUCTIONS

1. In bowl, combine turkey, mayonnaise, carrots, walnuts, celery and lemon zest. Season with salt and pepper. Set aside.

2. Place one slice sandwich bread on clean, flat surface; use rolling pin to flatten. Repeat with remaining bread. Set aside.

3. Lay arugula leaves onto flattened bread, leaving about 1/2-inch at end of each slice bare. Put layer of turkey-mayo mixture on top of arugula.

4. Roll tightly, then slice into bite-sized pieces.

LEFTOVER TURKEY CASSEROLE

SERVES 4–6 | PREP 18 MINS
COOK 30 MINS

INGREDIENTS

3 cups cooked turkey, chopped into bite-size pieces

1/2 cup celery, sliced

1/2 medium onion, chopped

1 can water chestnuts, sliced

1 can (10-1/2 ounces) cream of chicken soup

3/4 cup mayonnaise

3/4 teaspoon salt

1/2 teaspoon pepper

1 jar (4 ounces) pimientos, diced

1 cup potato chips, crushed, for topping

1 teaspoon ground paprika

INSTRUCTIONS

1. Preheat oven to 350F.

2. Mix all ingredients through pimientos and place in casserole dish.

3. Cover with crushed potato chips and sprinkle with paprika.

4. Bake uncovered for about 30 minutes, or until heated through and chips are lightly brown.

CHEESY BUFFALO TURKEY-STUFFED SHELLS

These cheesy Buffalo turkey-stuffed shells completely transform leftover turkey.

SERVES TBD | PREP 15 MINS | COOK 30 MINS

INGREDIENTS

2 cups leftover turkey,
finely chopped

4 tablespoons butter

1-1/2 cups Buffalo sauce, divided

2 tablespoons cream cheese

2 cups ricotta cheese

Salt, to taste

1 package jumbo pasta shells

1-1/2 cups Monterey jack
cheese, shredded

INSTRUCTIONS

1. Chop turkey and heat in large skillet. Set aside.

2. Melt butter in same skillet and stir in 1 cup Buffalo sauce. Add turkey again and stir until well combined.

3. Melt in cream cheese and remove from heat.

4. Stir in ricotta cheese. Add salt to taste.

5. Boil jumbo pasta shells according to package instructions to al dente.

6. Drain and allow to cool.

7. Stuff ricotta and turkey mixture into shells.

8. Arrange shells into 9-by-13-inch baking pan.

9. Top with 1/2 cup more Buffalo sauce. Cover evenly with shredded cheese.

10. Bake at 350F for 18 minutes.

11. If desired, top with more Buffalo sauce and enjoy immediately.

Food Gifts

CANDY-INFUSED VODKA

Here's an easy gift that combines the childhood love of sweet tastes and bright colors with an adults-only beverage: vodka!

(DF) (EF) (NF) (VG)

INGREDIENTS

1 liter vodka

2 pounds assorted hard fruit candies (around 50 candies)

INSTRUCTIONS

1. Separate candies by flavors.

2. Divide vodka among several flasks, 1 for each flavor of candy.

3. Drop candies of each flavor into each flask, adjusting candy/vodka ratios as desired. Start with about 25 pieces of candy for each half liter of vodka.

4. Using a funnel, pour vodka into the flasks, saturating the candies. Put the lids on the bottles.

5. Shake the bottles a few times throughout the day until candies have completely dissolved.

6. In only 24 hours, your infusion will be done and ready to drink.

7. Serve chilled for best flavor.

tip / Just about any candy that dissolves in liquid works for this gift.

HOMEMADE CARAMEL CORN

This homemade caramel popcorn can't be beat. It's addictive, easy to make and ready in less than an hour—perfect for last-minute holiday gifts.

INGREDIENTS

6 cups freshly popped popcorn (or plain microwave popcorn—no butter or other seasoning)

1/2 cup light corn syrup

1/4 cup water

2-3/4 cups sugar

1/2 tablespoon baking soda

8 tablespoons unsalted butter, cut into small pieces

1-1/2 tablespoons sea salt

INSTRUCTIONS

1. Line large baking sheet with parchment paper.

2. Spray pan, bowl and handle of large spoon or rubber spatula with nonstick cooking spray.

3. Transfer popped popcorn to large prepared bowl, discarding any unpopped kernels.

4. In large deep pot over moderately high heat, combine corn syrup, sugar and 1/4 cup water, stirring well to combine. Cook, undisturbed, until mixture develops light amber color, about 10 minutes.*

5. Remove pot from heat, add baking soda and butter, and stir continuously until butter is melted and well-combined.**

6. Immediately pour caramel over popcorn, then use prepared spoon or rubber spatula to stir.

7. Transfer from bowl to baking sheet. Spread caramel corn evenly over the sheet.

8. Sprinkle with sea salt and allow to cool and harden, at least 20 minutes.

9. Once cooled, break up caramel corn into bite-size pieces.

10. Serve or store in an airtight container for up to 3 days.

NOTES

*Once the sugar begins to caramelize, swirl the pan to evenly distribute the color, but don't stir. Stirring will cause the sugar to crystallize and harden.
**The mixture will be hot and will foam. Stir constantly until the foaming subsides.

HOMEMADE PEANUT BRITTLE

Make this beloved holiday candy from scratch. The taste will be far superior to store-bought varieties, so it's sure to delight any recipient.

INGREDIENTS

Canola oil, for greasing the slab

1/2 cup water

3/4 cup light corn syrup

2 cups sugar

1-1/2 cups raw peanuts (Spanish or blanched)

2 tablespoons unsalted butter, softened

1 teaspoon vanilla extract

3/4 teaspoon baking soda

1/2 teaspoon salt

INSTRUCTIONS

1. Place a marble slab, or inverted baking sheet, on the work space. Generously brush oil over the entire surface of the slab or sheet.

2. In a small bowl, sift together the baking soda and salt.

3. In a 4-quart deep, heavy-bottomed saucepan, combine the water, corn syrup and sugar. Stir over medium-low heat until the sugar dissolves, about 10 to 12 minutes.

4. Once the mixture is clear and begins to boil, increase the heat to high and stop stirring.

5. Place a candy thermometer in the mixture, holding it with an oven mitt to protect your hand. Cook until the syrup registers 265F on the thermometer, about 8 to 10 minutes.

6. Add the nuts and gently stir to incorporate.

7. Continue cooking, stirring occasionally, until the mixture reaches the hard-crack stage, 305F to 310F, about 5 minutes longer.

8. Immediately remove the pan from the heat.

9. Stir in the softened butter and vanilla extract, then the baking soda and salt. The mixture will soon start to foam.

10. Stir just until the mixture foams evenly and immediately pour it onto the oiled marble slab or inverted baking sheet.

11. The mixture should spread to about 14 inches in diameter.

12. Slip the oiled spatula under the hot candy to loosen the edges and bottom.

13. With gloved hands, and as soon as the candy is firm enough on the bottom to be picked up (the top won't be hard yet), lift the edges and turn the entire

piece of brittle over. Still wearing gloves, stretch the brittle so it's as thin as you can get it, about 17 inches in diameter.

14. Allow the candy to cool undisturbed for at least 1 hour and then break it into small pieces.

15. Store the brittle in airtight containers for up to 10 days.

HOT COCOA SHOTS

This festive DIY has a winning combination of flavor and charm. It's a perfect holiday gift for kids to make.

INGREDIENTS	INSTRUCTIONS
Glass favor jars	1. Using a teaspoon, fill jar about 1/3 full of cocoa mix.
Cocoa mix	2. Layer approximately 8-10 chocolate candies or chocolate chips on top of cocoa mix.
Mini marshmallows	3. Layer mini marshmallows on top of the candies and close jars.
Chocolate chips or chocolate candies	4. Tie decorative ribbon around jars.
Decorative ribbon for the bow	5. Don't forget to include directions: *To prepare the hot cocoa, empty into a small cup, mix with about 3.5 ounces (a little less than 1/2 cup) of hot water or milk.*

tip / Gifting to an adult? Add a mini liquor bottle for festive fun!

JAR OF CINNAMON AND SUGAR NUTS

These sweet and seasonal candied nuts make a perfect gift for neighbors, co-workers, hosts, or keep them for yourself.

INGREDIENTS

1 cup sugar

1 cup water

4 cups mixed nuts

2 tablespoons ground cinnamon

1 teaspoon salt

1 Mason jar

1 decorative ribbon

INSTRUCTIONS

1. In a medium saute pan over medium heat, combine sugar and water. Stir and cook until sugar is dissolved.

2. Pour in nuts and toss carefully to coat.

3. Cook, stirring constantly, about 5 minutes.

4. Stir in cinnamon and salt.

5. Remove from heat and pour into cake pan (or similar) to cool completely.

6. When cool, fill the Mason jar with the candied nuts.

7. Attach ribbon to jar.

MULLED WINE MIX

Cook this spice mix with red wine and it tastes like the grown-up cousin of hot mulled cider. Keep it on hand for festive entertaining or gift-giving.

DF EF GF GR NF **VG**

INGREDIENTS

2 tablespoons whole cloves

3 star anise pods

3 tablespoons dried orange peel

1/4 cup palm sugar

3 cinnamon sticks, broken in half

1 (750-milliliter) bottle red wine or grape juice

INSTRUCTIONS

1. Mix all spice ingredients together in bowl.

2. Place in clean, sterilized jar

3. Tie with ribbon and attach gift tag with instructions: *Empty the contents of the wine bottle and spice mix jar into a pot. Heat on medium until nearly boiling, but DO NOT boil. Heat for 30 minutes, then strain the mulled wine and return it to the pot. Add rum for additional flavor if desired.*

REINDEER CANDY BOTTLES

These crafty bottles filled with sweets are easy to make, don't cost a lot, and are super-cute and festive—in other words, they're perfect gifts for in a pinch.

SUPPLIES

Glass or plastic milk jars with lids

Brown chenille stems/ pipe cleaners

Malted milk balls or other brown candy

Googly eyes

Red fuzzy craft balls

INSTRUCTIONS

1. Tie brown chenille pipe cleaners around the top of the glass jar.
2. Cut one pipe cleaner in half and wrap around the end of the first pipe cleaner.
3. Repeat with other side and other pipe cleaner.
4. Fill jar with brown candy.
5. With a hot glue gun, affix googly eyes to the jar.
6. Glue the red fuzzy ball below the eyes.

SEA SALT VANILLA CARAMELS

Melt-in-your-mouth good, these caramels are topped with a sprinkling of coarse sea salt to provide just the right contrast to the sweetness. They're sure to bring a smile to any lucky recipient's face.

SUPPLIES

3/4 cup whipping cream

1 teaspoon vanilla

1/2 teaspoon kosher salt

4 tablespoons salted butter, softened

1 cup sugar

1/2 cup light corn syrup

1/4 teaspoon coarse sea salt

Clear jar and holiday ribbon, for gifting

INSTRUCTIONS

1. Line a 9-by-5-inch loaf pan with foil. Spray foil thoroughly with nonstick cooking spray.

2. Heat whipping cream, vanilla, kosher salt and 2 tablespoons butter in 2-quart saucepan over medium heat until mixture just starts to simmer. Remove from burner, cover with lid and set aside.

3. Mix sugar and corn syrup in 2-quart heavy saucepan and insert candy thermometer.

4. Stir gently over medium heat until sugar is completely dissolved. Use wet pastry brush to brush any stuck-on granules into syrup.

5. Continue to cook without stirring until thermometer reads 310F. Disperse any dark areas in the syrup by gently tilting the saucepan in a circular motion.

6. Remove pan from heat. Pour cream mixture into syrup gently and slowly to avoid boilover. Syrup will bubble vigorously.

7. Return pan to medium heat and continue to cook until candy thermometer reads 260F.

8. Remove thermometer. Remove pan from heat.

9. Stir in remaining 2 tablespoons butter. The caramel should look smooth.

10. Pour caramel into loaf pan and allow to cool for approximately 8 to 10 minutes.

11. Add sprinkling of coarse sea salt over top before completely cooling pan on cooling rack.

12. When caramel is completely cool, lift it from pan by grasping edges of foil and gently peeling it away from the caramel.

13. Cut into 35 to 40 squares with sharp knife. Wrap each caramel in twist of waxed paper and place in decorative tin tied with ribbon.

SPICED NUTS

These holiday spiced nuts offer a peppy take on traditional seasonal flavors. In a pretty jar, they make the perfect holiday gift and are sure to be a hit on any party table.

INGREDIENTS

5 tablespoons unsalted butter, melted

1/2 cup pure maple syrup

1/2 teaspoon ancho chili pepper

4 cups mixed nuts (whole almonds, pecans, walnuts, and/or pistachio nuts)

Coarse sea salt

2 teaspoons thyme, minced

2 teaspoons rosemary, minced

INSTRUCTIONS

1. Preheat oven to 325F.

2. In a large bowl, stir together the melted butter, maple syrup and ancho chili pepper.

3. Add the mixed nuts and toss well.

4. Prepare a baking tray with parchment paper and put the nuts on the tray.

5. Bake assorted nuts in oven for 20-25 minutes.

6. Remove tray of nuts from oven.

7. Combine fresh salt and fresh herbs in a small bowl.

8. Sprinkle herb mixture evenly over nuts.

9. Allow to cool, then serve.

tip / Ancho chili is mild and slightly sweet, but if you want a smoky flavor, try chipotle pepper or chile de arbol for a real punch of intense heat.

MINI CRANBERRY BREAD LOAVES

These easy holiday loaves are really more like moist, buttery mini-cakes bursting with sweet-tart cranberries, raisins and a hint of cinnamon.

INGREDIENTS

1-1/2 cups fresh cranberries

2 cups all-purpose white flour

1-1/2 teaspoons baking powder

1/2 teaspoon baking soda

1/4 teaspoon cinnamon

1/4 teaspoon ginger

1 teaspoon salt

1 cup sugar

1/4 cup cold butter, cut into 1/4-inch pieces

1 egg, beaten

3/4 cup orange juice

1 teaspoon orange rind, grated

1-1/2 cups golden raisins

1 gift bag

Holiday ribbon

INSTRUCTIONS

1. Chop cranberries coarsely by hand.

2. In a large bowl, combine and whisk flour, baking powder, baking soda, cinnamon, ginger, salt and sugar.

3. Mix butter into flour mixture with pastry blender until mixture is crumbly.

4. Add egg, orange juice and orange rind. Stir until ingredients are combined, but do not overmix.

5. Gently stir in cranberries and golden raisins.

6. Spoon batter into a greased and floured 4-cup mini-loaf pan.

7. Bake at 350F for 30-35 minutes or until a toothpick inserted in center comes out clean.

8. Allow bread to cool for 5 minutes.

9. Remove bread from pan and place on wire rack to continue cooling for 30 minutes.

10. Once cooled, insert in small gift bag, and tie with bow.

How Tos

HOW TO PLAN YOUR HOLIDAY

3 WEEKS AHEAD

☐ Write out your checklist of to-dos.

☐ Start planning your menu.

2 WEEKS AHEAD

☐ Finalize guest list, and ask for any dietary restrictions.

☐ Finalize menu, and assign dishes to guests. Write your grocery list and gather kitchen tools.

☐ Buy the turkey (stores can run out quickly).

☐ Gather glassware, dinnerware and utensils.

☐ Buy table decor.

tip / Borrow kitchen tools, glassware and tableware to save money.

1 WEEK AHEAD

☐ Purchase all menu ingredients.

SAME WEEK

☐ Prep your house: deep clean, plan table seating, and decorate.

☐ Thaw frozen turkey in fridge (1 day for every 4 lbs.).

tip / Use a cooler for beverages to free up fridge space.

3 DAYS AHEAD

☐ Set up the drink area.

tip / Stick to wine and one signature cocktail to keep things easy.

DAY BEFORE

☐ Bake the pies.

☐ Prep any make-ahead dishes.

☐ Cut any vegetables, fruits and cheeses for tomorrow's recipes.

☐ Set the table.

☐ Brine the turkey, if required.

☐ Determine what time you need to begin roasting your turkey the next day, and create a schedule for the rest of your recipes..

DAY OF

☐ In the morning, prep any slow-cooker dishes and do last minute clean-up.

☐ Assemble and begin cooking side dishes 2-3 hours before meal time.

☐ Wash dishes as you go (to save work later).

tip / If you're going casual, serve everything buffet style in the kitchen to save both table space and dirty serving dishes.

HOW TO STOCK YOUR PANTRY

These common pantry items will get you ready to prepare your holiday menu, but be sure to double-check your final recipes before starting prep to make sure you have all the ingredients you need.

BAKING GOODS

- [ ] Flour
- [ ] Sugars (brown, granulated and confectioners)
- [ ] Cornstarch
- [ ] Baking powder
- [ ] Baking soda
- [ ] Extracts (vanilla, almond)
- [ ] Honey
- [ ] Maple syrup
- [ ] Chocolate (unsweetened cocoa powder and semi-sweet chocolate chips)
- [ ] Canned milks (sweetened condensed and evaporated)

SPICES & SEASONINGS

- [ ] Sage
- [ ] Thyme
- [ ] Rosemary
- [ ] Poultry seasoning
- [ ] Bay leaf
- [ ] Pumpkin pie spice
- [ ] Nutmeg
- [ ] Cinnamon
- [ ] Cloves
- [ ] Salt and pepper

COOKING ESSENTIALS

- [ ] Nonstick cooking spray
- [ ] Olive oil
- [ ] Chicken stock
- [ ] Vegetable stock

NUTS & DRIED FRUITS

- [ ] Pecans
- [ ] Almonds
- [ ] Walnuts
- [ ] Raisins
- [ ] Dried cranberries
- [ ] Maraschino cherries

STARCHES

- [ ] Oats
- [ ] Bread crumbs
- [ ] Instant potatoes
- [ ] Dried pasta
- [ ] Rice
- [ ] Crackers (graham crackers and saltines)

CANNED & JARRED GOODS

- [ ] Canned corn
- [ ] Green beans
- [ ] Cranberry sauce
- [ ] Gravy
- [ ] Canned pumpkin

DRINKS

- [ ] Coffee
- [ ] Dried tea
- [ ] Hot chocolate mix
- [ ] Extra wine
- [ ] Bottled water

HOW TO ROAST A TURKEY

Roasting is one of the simplest, most popular ways to cook a turkey. Whether it's your first time or you're a pro, you can't go wrong using these no-fuss steps to perfectly roasting a turkey!

STEP 1: THAW THE TURKEY

Completely thaw the turkey. You can thaw it in the fridge for a few days or submerge it in cold water until thawed, changing the water every 30 minutes.

STEP 2: PREP THE TURKEY

- After rinsing and patting dry, let the turkey sit in the roasting pan on a roasting rack at room temperature for 1-2 hours, breast side up.
- Preheat the oven to 400F.
- Rub your turkey with butter or oil and seasonings. The butter or oil will help create the crisp, brown skin everyone loves!

STEP 3: PLACE THE TURKEY IN OVEN

- If you're going to stuff the turkey, do so immediately before placing it in the oven. Once the oven is preheated, place the turkey in the roasting pan in the oven on the lowest rack.
- Immediately lower the temperature to 325F.

STEP 4: COOK THE TURKEY

- After your turkey has been cooking for an hour and a half, check the temperature.
- When it reaches 180F in the thigh and 165F in the breast (and stuffing), your turkey is done.
- If the skin seems to be getting too brown, cover it with aluminum foil and continue cooking.
- If you're basting your turkey, do so every 30 minutes, but it's not necessary for a brown skin. The key to a moist turkey isn't the basting—it's ensuring you don't overcook it!

STEP 5: REST AND CARVE THE TURKEY

Once it's fully cooked, remove it from the oven and let it rest for at least 30 minutes before carving. This will keep all the juices from pouring out when you cut it. "Tent" your turkey with aluminum foil while it rests to keep it from drying out and to make it easier to carve.

HOW TO DEEP FRY A TURKEY

Roasting has long been the traditional way to prepare turkey. But for the brave, frying can create a juicy, perfectly browned turkey that oozes with delicious flavor.

STEP 1: GET THE EQUIPMENT

You will need a turkey, a turkey fryer, and a lot of oil (peanut oil is recommended).

STEP 2: PREP THE TURKEY

- Completely thaw the turkey. You can thaw it in the fridge for a few days or submerge it in cold water until thawed, changing the water every 30 minutes.

- Once thawed, pat the turkey dry and remove the neck and giblets from the cavity. Sprinkle the turkey with your choice of seasonings, such as salt, pepper, poultry seasoning, and paprika.

- Allow the turkey to sit at room temperature for an hour or two before frying.

STEP 3: PREHEAT THE FRYER

Set up the fryer outside and on a noncombustible surface, such as concrete or brick. Slowly pour the oil into the deep fryer, making sure not to fill the oil higher than the maximum fill line. While any vegetable oil will work, peanut oil is best for frying turkeys. Preheat the oil to 375F.

STEP 4: COOKING THE TURKEY

- Slowly and carefully lower the turkey into the preheated oil so it's submerged. (If parts of the turkey aren't submerged, that's okay. It will still cook properly.)

- Your turkey will probably need 3 to 4 minutes of frying time per pound. Once the dark meat reaches 180F and the white meat reaches 170F, your turkey is done.

STEP 5: COOL AND REST THE TURKEY

- As soon as the internal temperatures have been reached, turn the burner off. Carefully raise your turkey out of the oil and place it onto paper towels to drain.

- Allow the turkey to rest for 30 minutes.

STEP 6: CARVE AND ENJOY!

Carve the turkey and savor the moist, succulent meat along with your other favorite Thanksgiving sides.

HOW MUCH SHOULD YOU SERVE?

TURKEY	POTATOES AND VEGGIE SIDE DISHES	PIE
5 people = 8 pounds	5 people = 2.5 pounds	5 people = 2 pies
10 people = 15 pounds	10 people = 4 pounds	10 people = 3 pies
15 people = 20 pounds	15 people = 6 pounds	15 people = 4 pies
20 people = 25 pounds	20 people = 8 pounds	20 people = 5 pies

HELPFUL HINTS

- 1 stick of butter = 8 tablespoons = 1/2 cup
- One 9x13 casserole dish = 8 servings
- 1 packet of yeast = 2-½ teaspoons
- 1 lemon = 2 tablespoons lemon juice
- Don't use liquid measuring cups for dry ingredients, though you can use dry measuring cups for liquids.
- Measuring spoons can be used for either dry or wet ingredients.
- Packing is the standard way brown sugar (but only brown sugar) is measured for all recipes.
- Coat measuring utensils with cooking spray before filling with sticky substances such as honey, agave or maple syrup to help it slide out with ease.

HOW TO CONVERT MEASUREMENTS

½ TABLESPOON = 1-½ TEASPOONS

1 TABLESPOON = 3 TEASPOONS

⅛ CUP = 2 TABLESPOONS = 1 OUNCE

¼ CUP = 4 TABLESPOONS = 2 OUNCES

⅓ CUP = 5 TABLESPOONS + 1 TEASPOON

½ CUP = 8 TABLESPOONS = 4 OUNCES

⅔ CUP = 10 TABLESPOONS + 2 TEASPOONS

¾ CUP = 12 TABLESPOONS = 6 OUNCES

1 CUP = 16 TABLESPOONS = 8 OUNCES = ½ PINT

2 CUPS = 1 PINT

4 CUPS = 2 PINTS = 32 OUNCES = 1 QUART

DIETARY INDEX

	PAGE	DAIRY-FREE	EGG-FREE	GLUTEN-FREE	GRAIN-FREE	LOW-CARB	NUT-FREE	QUICK	VEGETARIAN	VEGAN
Baked Brie with blackberry compote and pecans	24		•						•	
Beef meatballs with zesty cranberry cocktail sauce	34						•			
Caramelized onion and spinach stuffed mushrooms	38		•	•					•	
Charcuterie board	40									
Cheesy prosciutto-wrapped asparagus bundles	39		•	•	•	•	•	•		
Divine guacamole dip	20	•	•	•	•	•	•	•	•	•
Easy bacon jalapeño cheese ball	32		•							
Elegant crab dip	18		•				•			
Garlicky pumpkin hummus	27	•		•	•		•		•	•
Homemade wonton crackers	28	•					•	•	•	
Mini 7-layer dips	21		•	•			•	•	•	
Pressure cooker artichoke and spinach dip	22			•		•			•	
Spicy mini bacon cheese balls	30		•							
Spinach artichoke deviled eggs	16			•			•		•	
Tuna tartare	29	•	•	•			•			
Turkey cranberry meatballs	36									
Vegan raw "cheese" sun-dried tomato and pesto spread	26	•	•	•	•	•			•	•
Autumn kale and spinach salad	50		•	•	•		•		•	
Beet, apple and orange salad	50	•	•	•					•	
Celery root, apple and walnut salad	51	•						•	•	
Citrus, berry and feta salad	48		•	•					•	
Holiday salad with arugula and cranberries	51		•	•					•	
Pear salad with blood orange vinaigrette	52		•	•					•	
Red wine grape, tangerine and wild rice salad	47	•	•	•					•	
Shredded Brussels sprouts, apple and walnut salad	44		•	•					•	
Smoky quinoa black bean salad	46	•	•	•			•		•	•
Cream of kale soup with parmesan crisps	57		•	•	•	•	•		•	
Creamy onion soup with bacon nut crumble	53		•	•	•					
Slow-cooker French onion and sweet potato soup	56		•				•			
Slow-cooker roasted garlic baked potato soup	54		•	•	•		•			
Vegan cauliflower soup	55	•	•	•	•	•			•	•
Best basic dinner rolls	66		•				•		•	
Cornucopia bread basket	76		•				•		•	
Gluten-free cornbread with cherry butter	74			•			•		•	
Grandma's Southern buttermilk biscuits	64						•		•	
Honey cornbread muffins	60						•	•	•	
Homemade no-knead bread	75		•				•		•	
Keto cauliflower bread	72	•		•	•	•			•	
Orange cranberry muffins	62						•		•	
Rosemary-maple cornbread muffins	66		•				•		•	
Sweet potato biscuits	67		•				•		•	

DIETARY INDEX
(continued)

	PAGE	DAIRY-FREE	EGG-FREE	GLUTEN-FREE	GRAIN-FREE	LOW-CARB	NUT-FREE	QUICK	VEGETARIAN	VEGAN
Twisted rosemary breadsticks	70	•	•				•	•	•	•
Whole wheat dinner rolls with pumpkin seeds	68		•				•		•	
Balsamic and parmesan roasted cauliflower	93			•	•	•	•			
Brandied wild rice stuffing with cornbread and pecans	110		•	•						
Cauliflower mashed potatoes with Swiss chard	91		•	•	•		•		•	
Chunky mashed potatoes	86		•	•	•		•		•	
Creamy baked macaroni and cheese	101						•			
Gluten-free, paleo green bean casserole	97	•	•	•	•	•			•	
Grain-free stuffing	106	•	•	•					•	
Green beans with crunchy almonds	94	•	•					•		•
Gruyere, ham and onion stuffing	108						•			
Honey butter roasted acorn squash	118		•	•	•		•		•	
Honey cinnamon sweet potatoes	82		•	•	•		•		•	
Keto stuffing	104					•				
Maple bacon roasted Brussels sprouts	112	•	•				•			
Mushroom stuffing	109	•	•	•						•
Pressure cooker green bean casserole	96								•	
Pressure cooker mac and cheese	102						•			
Roasted butternut squash	116	•	•	•	•		•		•	
Roasted carrots with Indian spices	114		•	•	•		•		•	
Roasted poblano creamed corn	92		•	•			•		•	
Scalloped potatoes	90		•				•		•	
Slow-cooker million-dollar mashed potatoes	88		•	•	•		•			
Sour cream, cheddar and chive mashed potatoes	84		•	•	•		•			
Southern green beans with roasted garlic	100		•	•	•	•	•			
Vegan green bean casserole	98	•	•						•	•
Bacon-wrapped turkey	124		•	•	•		•			
Cajun-spiced deep fried turkey	123		•	•	•	•	•			
Classic roasted turkey	132		•				•			
Easy no-fuss Thanksgiving turkey	134		•	•	•		•			
Mayonnaise roasted turkey	128			•	•	•	•			
Orange bourbon slow-cooker turkey breast	130	•	•				•			
Orange, anise and thyme roasted turkey	136		•	•	•		•			
Rosemary lemon roasted turkey	126		•							
Rosemary turkey breast roasted in oven bag	122		•	•	•	•	•			
Creamy salmon piccata	156		•				•			
Garlic herb-crusted roast beef	144	•	•	•	•	•	•			
Grilled salmon with maple and rosemary	158	•	•	•	•		•	•		
Honey glazed baked ham	152		•	•	•		•			
Orange pepper glazed baked ham	154	•	•	•	•		•			
Pan-seared filet mignon with shallot butter	148		•		•	•	•			

DIETARY INDEX
(continued)

	PAGE	DAIRY-FREE	EGG-FREE	GLUTEN-FREE	GRAIN-FREE	LOW-CARB	NUT-FREE	QUICK	VEGETARIAN	VEGAN
Pork tenderloin with sweet and spicy rub	150	•	•	•	•		•			
Roast pork loin with dried fruits	151	•	•				•			
Slow-cooked prime rib with horseradish cream sauce	146		•	•	•		•			
Tofurkey with mushroom stuffing and gravy	138	•	•						•	•
Vegan butternut roast	162	•	•	•	•				•	•
Vegetable Wellington	160						•			
Apple cranberry sauce	174	•	•				•	•	•	•
Best basic pan gravy	175	•	•				•	•	•	
Cranberry bacon gravy	174	•	•	•			•			
Crunchy cranberry sauce	170	•	•				•		•	
Homemade orange cranberry sauce	166	•	•				•		•	•
Jalapeño cranberry sauce	172	•	•				•		•	•
Lemon and rosemary turkey gravy	178	•	•	•			•	•		
Turkey-onion gravy	176	•	•				•	•		
Vanilla bourbon balsamic cranberry sauce	168	•	•				•		•	•
Brownie chocolate chip cookie dough bars	220						•			
Black bean brownies	190		•	•			•	•		
Chocolate-Kahlua snowball cookies	216	•						•	•	•
Cranberry almond pie	198								•	
Dark chocolate pecan pie	182								•	
Gluten free and vegan ground nut pie crust	212	•	•	•	•				•	•
Grain-free pecan pie	201			•	•				•	
Healthy vegan chocolate pecan pie	196	•	•						•	
Holiday cheese tart with strawberry glaze	208						•		•	
Holiday mixed fruit pie	192			•			•		•	
No-bake coconut date balls	217						•	•	•	
No-bake pumpkin pie	203		•				•		•	
Peppermint Mocha Cookies	184						•		•	
Pressure cooker salted caramel cheesecake	206						•		•	
Pumpkin cheesecake parfaits	202		•				•	•	•	
Pumpkin pecan cheesecake bars	222								•	
Pumpkin pie with harvest spiced almonds	204								•	
Pumpkin roll with cream cheese filling	226						•		•	
Red velvet cream cheese cookie sandwiches	188						•	•	•	
Skillet apple pie	194						•		•	
Soda shoppe sugar cookies	214						•		•	
Sweet potato cake with marshmallow frosting	224								•	
Sweet potato pie	186						•		•	
Traditional pie crust	210		•				•		•	
Truffles three ways	218								•	
Vegan whipped cream	197	•	•	•			•	•	•	•

DIETARY INDEX
(continued)

	PAGE	DAIRY-FREE	EGG-FREE	GLUTEN-FREE	GRAIN-FREE	LOW-CARB	NUT-FREE	QUICK	VEGETARIAN	VEGAN
Apple cider sangria	239	•	•	•	•		•	•	•	•
Amaretto cranberry kiss	235	•	•						•	•
Boozy pumpkin white hot chocolate	243		•				•		•	
Chocolate espresso martini	234		•				•		•	
Dulce de Leche hot chocolate	246		•	•	•		•		•	
Holiday orange wassail punch	240	•	•				•		•	
Holiday-spiced sangria	238	•	•				•		•	
Hot apple cider with buttered rum	248		•	•	•		•		•	
Jalapeño cranberry cosmos	234	•	•				•		•	•
Orangecello and honey martini	232	•	•				•		•	
Peppermint white Russian cocktail	233		•				•		•	
Pomegranate thyme bubbly rosé	235	•	•	•			•		•	
Pumpkin fizz cocktail	244	•	•				•		•	
Rich mocha eggnog	230						•		•	
Simple maple bacon eggnog	233						•			
Sweet and fruity faux champagne	242	•	•	•			•		•	•
Toasted hot chocolate	232		•	•					•	
Vegan spiced-apple margaritas	236	•	•				•		•	•
Cheesy Buffalo turkey-stuffed shells	269						•			
Holiday leftovers poppers	260									
Leftovers pastry pockets	267									
Leftover turkey casserole	268	•					•			
Leftover turkey chili smothered sweet potatoes	262		•	•			•			
Leftover turkey enchiladas	258		•				•			
Leftover turkey pinwheel sandwiches	268							•		
Leftover turkey pot pie soup	264		•	•				•		
Leftover turkey shepherd's pie	252		•	•	•					
Leftover turkey taquitos with nutty Buffalo dipping sauce	256		•							
Turkey "carnitas" tacos	254	•	•				•			
Candy-infused vodka	272	•	•				•		•	•
Homemade caramel corn	274								•	
Homemade peanut brittle	276		•	•					•	
Hot cocoa shots	278		•	•					•	
Jar of cinnamon and sugar nuts	279	•	•	•	•				•	•
Mini cranberry bread loaves	285						•		•	
Mulled wine mix	280	•	•	•	•		•		•	
Reindeer candy bottles	281		•				•		•	
Sea salt vanilla caramels	282		•				•		•	
Spiced nuts	284		•	•					•	

INDEX

GUEST CONTRIBUTORS

We'd like to extend a special thank you to these Grateful family food bloggers who generously contributed some of their favorite holiday recipes and gorgeous photography to this collection.

JESSICA GAVIN

jessicagavin.com

BIO

Jessica Gavin uses her superpowers, which include degrees and certifications in agriculture, culinary science and food science, to help her readers get smart about getting dinner on the table. Her work has been featured by The Food Network, the Kitchn, BuzzFeed and more.

RECIPES

Green beans with crunchy almonds *(94)*
Homemade orange cranberry sauce *(166)*
Honey cornbread muffins *(60)*

| jessica_gavin | f jessicayeegavin | jessica_gavin | foodiegavin |

KATIE HIGGINS

chocolatecoveredkatie.com

BIO

Food blogger and cookbook author Katie has been hailed as the "queen of healthy desserts" by Glamour Magazine, was named one of The Huffington Post's best healthy food instagram accounts to follow and has been featured by The Today Show, USA Today, The Food Network and Cooking Light.

RECIPES

Black bean brownies *(190)*
Roasted butternut squash *(116)*

| chocolatecoveredkatie | f chocolatecoveredkatie | choccoveredkt |

MONIQUE KILGORE

divascancook.com

BIO

Monique is committed to making down-home Southern recipes less intimidating and even more tasty for your table with her coveted family recipes. A new voice in Southern cooking, Monique's recipes have been praised by Nate Berkus, Curtis Stone, Dr. Oz and Jessica Alba.

RECIPES

Creamy baked macaroni and cheese *(101)*
Red velvet cream cheese cookies sandwiches *(188)*
Sweet potato pie *(186)*

⊙ divascancook   f divascancookfanpage   🐦 divascancook   𝓟 divascancook

SALLY MCKENNEY

sallysbakingaddiction.com

BIO

Sally is a cookbook author, photographer and blogger behind Sally's Baking Addiction - a trusted resource for fellow dessert lovers who are eager to bake from scratch. Sally has developed hundreds of from-scratch recipes inspired by seasonal favorites and recipes that have been passed down to her.

RECIPES

Dark chocolate pecan pie *(182)*
Peppermint mocha cookies *(184)*
Apple cider sangria *(239)*

⊙ sallysbakeblog   f sallysbakingaddiction   🐦 sallysbakeblog   𝓟 sallysbakeblog

ACKNOWLEDGMENTS

They say it takes a village to raise a child. Well, we have found that it takes a village to create a cookbook, too. The one you hold in your hands is the culmination of more than a year's worth of work by recipe developers and chefs, writers and editors, photographers and graphic designers, and many others dedicated to bringing you delicious kitchen-tested recipes we hope you will be proud to make your own.

Like any memorable holiday meal, this cookbook was a labor of love by our Thanksgiving.com team. We are grateful for our bloggers, contributors and test-kitchen team for ensuring these recipes are worthy of America's tables.

HERE'S WHO HELPED MAKE IT ALL HAPPEN:

COOKBOOK CONTENT & DESIGN TEAM: Kyle Cox, Amy Nichols, Betsy Bailey, Kristin Bustamante, Tiffany Egbert, Luis Espinosa, Ashley Scott, Stronz Vanderploeg, David Flores, Jim Cox, Christina Haller, Kimberlee Bradford, Allison Yoder, Vanessa Sands, Denise Long, Jen Klein, Rita Loiacano

THANKSGIVING.COM EDITORIAL TEAM: Nancy J. Price, Christine McDow, Lauren Joskowitz, Michele Borboa Stafford, Stephanie Koebel, Lori Blevins, Shannon Dufresne, Mary Lebeau, Monica Beyer, Jessica Wilhelmsen, Lola Hunt

THANKSGIVING.COM TEST KITCHEN CREW: Debbie Elder, Lori Ann Harnish, Peggy McMahon, Molly Edwards, Bridget Dwyer, Elena O'Brien, Jess Suworoff

THANKSGIVING.COM STUDIO CREW: Ashlyn Jean Axelsen, Tiberius Cătinaș, Elizabeth Tinajero, Tyler Tang, Morgan Callahan, Samantha Sausedo, Chuck Sterling, Reid Bard, Tyler Schneider, Quinlan Donovan-Schager, Caden DePietro

Thanksgiving.com is part of Grateful Ventures, an online media company that builds and supports food and lifestyle brands; and the USA TODAY Network, which helps us bring our most cherished recipes to more tables across America than ever. We would like to thank our many colleagues across the Network, as well as the hundreds of food bloggers (too many to name) who inspire and collaborate with us. We are incredibly fortunate to be working with such a talented crew of doers and creators.

Finally, we are grateful for you, our readers. We hope these recipes and cooking tips will help make your holiday gatherings shine. For many more recipes for Thanksgiving, Christmas and beyond, please visit Thanksgiving.com—America's home for the holidays.